www.hants.gov.uk/library

Tel: 0300 555 1387

 Hampshire
County Council

 Love
YOUR LIBRARY

VEGAN FOOD
RECIPES & PREPARATION

The information in this book should not be treated as a substitute for professional medical advice. Neither the author nor the publisher can be held responsible for any claim or damage arising out of the use, or misuse, of the information and suggestions made in this book.

Saskia Fraser is an expert on veganism and raw food. As an author and lifestyle coach she has helped thousands of busy working women to experience greater energy, mental clarity and self-confidence. Saskia runs raw food detoxes and workshops, in person and online, as well as one-to-one life-coaching programmes. She is the author of *Raw Freedom*, a raw food recipe book for busy lives, as well as a popular raw food blog.

Publisher & Creative Director: Nick Wells
Senior Project Editor: Catherine Taylor
Copy Editor: Kathy Steer
Art Director: Mike Spender
Layout Design: Jane Ashley
Digital Design & Production: Chris Herbert
Proofreader: Dawn Laker

Special thanks to Laura Bulbeck, Gillian Whitaker, Carly Laird and Josh Vitchkoski

FLAME TREE PUBLISHING
6 Melbray Mews, Fulham,
London SW6 3NS, United Kingdom
www.flametreepublishing.com

This edition published 2017

ISBN: 978-1-78664-478-7

Printed in China

Picture Credits
© Stockfood and the following: 80 Koene, Robbert; 110 Firmston, Victoria; 121 Studio Lipov; 131, 211, 221 Hendey, Magdalena; 133, 156 Gräfe & Unzer Verlag / Zanin, Melanie; 137 Paul, Michael; 145 Gräfe & Unzer Verlag / Schardt, Wolfgang; 155 Short, Jonathan; 179 Parissi, Lucy; 181 Pizzochero, Franco; 187 Eising Studio - Food Photo & Video; 188 Garlick, Ian; 201 Castilho, Rua; 208 The Picture Pantry; 215 Morgans, Gareth. Courtesy Shutterstock.com and the following: 44 Adisa; 48l, 55b, 64r, 74, 123 Africa Studio; 92 & 224 AlenaKogotkova; 9tl, 78 alexpro9500; 4 AllAnd; 57t Alliance; 47b Amawasri Pakdara; 52b Ana Photo; 192 Anchiy; 55tl Andrii Vodolazhskyi; 89 & back cover top right Anna Kurzaeva; 191 Anna Shepulova; 165 Anna_Pustynnikova; 9tr, 73 AS Food studio; 7, 35l baibaz; 175 bonchan; 19br & back cover bottom left, 20t, 38t, 138, 172 Brent Hofacker; 134 casanisa; 52t Cegli; 64l daylightistanbul studio; 27bl Degtiarova Viktoriia; 66t DenisFilm; 58tl Dragon Images; 61tr Edith Frincu; 109 Ekaterina Kondratova; 69t, 176 Elena Veselova; 207 Family Business; 3 Flaffy; 27br FooTToo; 61br fotolotos; 55tr Foxxy63; 96 Foxys Forest Manufacture; 49l HandmadePictures; 219 hd connelly; 167 Ievgeniia Maslovska; 9b Igabriela; 61tl Ina Ts; 19t iprachenko; 91 Jayme Burrows; 49r JOAT; 171 Joshua Resnick; 25 JRP Studio; 51t Julia Sudnitskaya; 29l Jurga Jot; 116 K2 PhotoStudio; 125 Kati Molin; 37t Kerdkanno; 99 Kiian Oksana; 28r kolo5; 33t kurhan; 65r Leszek Glasner; 103 Liliya Kandrashevich; 168 & back cover top left Lilyana Vynogradova; 51br Looker_Studio; 148, 159 & front cover marco mayer; 194 Maria Komar; 95 Maria Shumova; 29r Maridav; 34 Micolas; 217 Mshev; 48r mythja; 153 natalia bulatova; 6br, 129 Nataliya Arzamasova; 77 Natasha Breen; 17b Nemanja Novakovic; 100 Nikolaev Mikhail; 66bl Nitr; 69br ocphoto; 150 Oko Laa; 141 Oleg B-art; 14t Oleksandra Naumenko; 118 Olena Kaminetska; 161 Olexiy Bayev; 24r Operation Shooting; 27t pan demin; 47tl Peangdao; 14b photographyfirm; 24l Pikoso.kz; 23, 33b Pressmaster; 197 Razmarinka; 57br Rob Byron; 41b Robert Przybysz; 65l Robyn Mackenzie; 38bl Roman Boiko; 62 S_Photo; 6bl saschanti17; 69bl showcake; 61bl Shyripa Alexandr; 199 Soumitra Pendse; 58b Stephen Gibson; 51bl Syda Productions; 17t symbiot; 83 tacar; 113 Tatiana Bralnina; 85 Tatiana Vorona; 58tr, 205 thefoodphotographer; 13t Timolina; 185 & back cover bottom right Ulyana Khorunzha; 20b vaaseenaa; 41t Valeria Aksakova; 42 Vasyl90; 105 VICUSCHKA; 147 Virginia Garcia; 19bl VISCUSCHKA; 28l Vladimir Voronchenko; 1, 13br Vorontsova Anastasiia; 13bl Y Photo Studio; 37b yesyesterday; 47tr yingko; 212 Yulia Davidovich; 30 Yulia Grigoryeva; 38br Yunava1; 115 zarzamora; 35r Zholobov Vadim; 66br zi3000; 57bl Zigzag Mountain Art; and small watercolour illustrations throughout: Le Panda and Paket.

VEGAN FOOD
RECIPES & PREPARATION

Saskia Fraser

FLAME TREE
PUBLISHING

CONTENTS

INTRODUCTION

Veganism is growing in popularity, and with good reason. Vegan recipes not only taste delicious but are good for the planet and for our conscience. Specialist cruelty-free products are becoming available everywhere, and more restaurants are offering vegan options. Today, making this ethical lifestyle choice is becoming easier and easier.

HOW TO USE THIS BOOK

This recipe book is a guide and inspiration. What does it mean to be vegan? Which foods are considered vegan? What is a vegan 'lifestyle'? Find out in the section What is Vegan?

Have you heard that vegan food is boring, or unhealthy? Sure, if you only eat lettuce, or load up too much on nuts; but in reality it can easily be excitingly tasty, vibrant and great for you. The section on Busting the Myths gives you the lowdown.

Veganism is a great choice, not just morally and ethically but for your health too. Find out more in the section Why Vegan?

What's the best way to transition to a cruelty-free way of life? I show you how in the section Making the Transition.

Check out the section on Key Vegan Foods for all the delicious ingredients you can eat as a vegan.

Find out what kit is especially useful for a vegan cook in the section on Tools & Equipment, and finally, learn how to prepare and cook vegan food in our section on Preparation & Techniques.

THE RECIPES

Day to Day

The recipes in this book have been created for healthy, comforting and creative eating. You will find staple vegan recipes, including how to make your own dairy-free milks, custard, yogurt and ice cream. Not only is it fun to make your own, but if you like cooking, you can avoid less tasty, store-bought alternatives that contain additives.

Have fun exploring the inspiring breakfasts, brunches and smoothies that will kickstart your day with energy and deliciousness. Lunch needs to be quick, easy and often portable, so that's what there is a section on Light Meals & Sides, which includes salads, sandwiches and soups to keep you satisfied.

The Main Event

When it's time for comfort food, try the Cauliflower Mac 'n' Cheeze (*see* page 168) or Spaghetti with Meatless Balls (*see* page 178), and when you are in need of a snack then try the tasty dips and recipes like Nacho Popcorn on page 140.

If you want to have a vegan dinner party, or make a special meal for two, check out the Thai Green Curry (*see* page 184), Potato Dauphinoise (*see* page 194), Spanakopita (*see* page 200) and more. No one will miss the meat!

Sweet Fix

When you want to treat yourself, family and friends, the Cakes, Treats & Desserts section will inspire you with delicious recipes, such as the Shortbread (*see* page 212), Chocolate Fudge Cake (*see* page 214) or the Sticky Mango Rice Pudding (*see* page 218).

WHAT IS VEGAN?

A BRIEF HISTORY OF VEGANISM

Veganism has seen a huge surge in popularity since the 1970s. It is a fuller expression of vegetarianism, and is an ethical lifestyle choice. Someone who takes on the mantle of 'vegan' aims to ensure no animals are harmed by their choices. There is evidence of the deliberate avoidance of animal products dating back over 2000 years. Around 500 BC, Pythagoras was promoting a benevolence among all species and eating in accordance with his values. About the same time, Buddha was teaching vegetarian principles – having compassion for the animals of our planet, and therefore not eating them – to his followers.

The Vegan Movement

Modern day veganism began as a more developed version of vegetarianism in 1944, when Donald Watson decided that 'vegetarian' did not adequately describe his diet and lifestyle choices and, along with a group of six other non-dairy vegetarians, coined the term 'vegan'.

Today

Nowadays, many people are choosing veganism for health reasons as well as reasons of conscience. Many famous actors, models and pop stars are choosing and promoting veganism, and it has also become a fashionable lifestyle choice. World Vegan Day is 1 November, when veganism is celebrated and championed all over the world.

VEGANISM DEFINED

Veganism in its broadest sense is the choice to live a cruelty-free lifestyle. For some, this only applies to food choices. For others, it extends to their clothes, cosmetics, household products and anything else that may have caused harm to an animal. The first official definition of veganism was created in 1949 as 'The principle of the emancipation of animals from exploitation by man'. After a few more clarifications over the years, the Vegan Society's official definition of veganism is now: 'A philosophy and way of living which seeks to exclude – as far as is possible and practicable – all forms of exploitation of, and cruelty to, animals for food, clothing or any other purpose; and by extension, promotes the development and use of animal-free alternatives for the benefit of humans, animals and the environment. In dietary terms it denotes the practice of dispensing with all products derived wholly or partly from animals.'

What Vegans Eat

Being a vegan means that you don't eat animal products: no meat; no fish; no eggs; no dairy products, such as cheese, milk, yogurt, whey or butter; no bee products, such as honey, bee pollen or propolis; no gelatine, or anything else that comes from, is made by or includes an animal.

What Vegans Wear

If you choose to take the vegan principles further into your life, this will mean no leather shoes, belts or clothing; no woollen clothes or accessories; and no accessories made from shells, pearls or feathers, or anything else that comes from, is made by or includes an animal.

Cosmetics

By fully embracing a vegan lifestyle you choose to be conscious of and conscientious about everything you use in your life. The vast majority of ingredients in beauty and bathroom products are tested on animals. Check that cosmetics, shampoos, conditioners, moisturizers, cleansers, toners and hair dyes are marked 'cruelty-free' before you buy them.

Household Products

Washing up liquid, laundry detergent, fabric conditioner, bleach, household cleaners, air fresheners and upholstery cleaners are another area where animal testing is widely used. Glues and wax often contain animal products. Do your research to find out which brands are not tested on animals and look for the vegan mark.

Modern Versus Traditional Veganism

Veganism used to be seen as very extreme and limiting, with a 'holier-than-though' image. However, over the last decade many inspiring and creative vegans have turned this image around. Veganism has now filtered into top restaurants and is being made more popular by celebrities and high-profile chefs. Plant-based is the new cool!

BUSTING THE MYTHS

'VEGAN FOOD IS BLAND & BORING'

Vegan food can be boring, just like any other kind of food, but it can also be delicious. Vegan flavours are rich, deep, fresh, light, spicy, complex, simple and sophisticated, and ingredients can be local, international or exotic. Whatever your preferences, there is a world of exciting vegan recipes to explore.

Get Ready for a Taste Sensation!

Vegan recipes used to have a reputation for being 'brown bread and beans', but today there is worldwide inspiration and flavours are at your fingertips. Whether you love hearty stews, Thai curries, Italian-inspired salads or Mexican food, there is plenty to get excited about.

Vegan Ingredients

Vegan ingredients are plentiful and easy to find everywhere. With a few simple elements, you can make something in minutes that tastes amazing. And, if you want to spend time in the kitchen, you can create serious comfort food or a sophisticated dinner party dish worthy of royalty.

Cutting Out Meat & Cheese

If you are new to being vegan, you may wonder how exciting food can be without meat, fish, eggs and cheese. Let me assure you, it won't be long before you don't miss the taste of animal ingredients at all. Plus, vegan cheese and meat substitutes are now readily available.

Top: Smoked tofu 'cheese'; Far right: Pulled jackfruit 'burger'

'VEGANISM IS NOT HEALTHY FOR YOU'

There is a myth that getting the right nutrition is not possible on a vegan diet. Of course, it is possible to be an unhealthy vegan, as it is to be an unhealthy meat-eater, but there are numerous studies showing that a flesh-free diet can in fact be better for you.

Where to Get Your Nutrition

As a healthy vegan, it is important to know where to get certain nutrients on a plant-based diet. Meat is a major source of iron, while eggs and dairy are the standard dietary source of B12. Take a closer look at nutrition in the section on transitioning to a vegan lifestyle.

Junk Veganism

It is very easy to be a 'junk vegan'. Many unhealthy processed, pre-packaged and fast food options are available. An uninformed vegan can easily end up living off bread, pasta, fries and vegan cheese, while being frustrated that they have pimples and that they are putting on weight.

Real Food Veganism

Being a real-food vegan means that you take care of yourself, as well as the animals on the planet, by eating whole food ingredients that nourish, energize and replenish you. It means using lots of fresh veggies and fruit as well as the plethora of other plant-based ingredients that are available.

'BEING VEGAN IS TIME-CONSUMING & DIFFICULT'

In transitioning to a vegan diet, many people take longer than they would like to because they think it is time-consuming and difficult. While it's true that you need to learn new ways of cooking and be more mindful when eating out or eating with friends, it can also simplify life.

Vegan Recipes

Vegan recipes can be super easy without compromising on flavour. You can whizz up a salad, soup or sandwich in minutes. Cruelty-free recipes are no more difficult or time-consuming than any other kind of recipes, and are a great opportunity to expand your recipe repertoire while loving the planet.

Eating with Friends & Family

Have fun! Impress your friends and family with the kinds of recipes that are possible without using animal products. Have vegan dinner parties or relaxed weekend lunches as a way of introducing them to the deliciousness of plant-based eating. Keep them in their comfort zone by trying recipes that look like traditional recipes, but without the animal products.

Eating Out

Eating out as a vegan is becoming a lot easier. Research which restaurants offer vegan dishes, as well as seeking out dedicated vegan locations. If you find yourself at a place without vegan options, ask for something special. Not all chefs understand what is and isn't vegan, so be explicit.

'VEGANISM IS ABOUT DENIAL'

There is no need to worry about what you are giving up by becoming vegan. There are many talented people in the vegan world, pushing the boundaries of what is possible on a plant-based diet. With recipes like egg- and dairy-free pancakes (see pages 88 and 204), vegan cheesecake (see page 206) and spaghetti with meatless balls (see page 178), who needs denial?

Vegan Dairy Substitutes

People often think they will miss dairy products when they go vegan. Luckily, there are delicious, cruelty-free alternatives that make letting go of dairy easy. There are plenty of recipes for fresh, plant-based milks, cheeses and yogurt, as well as pre-packaged options for when you want 'melty' cheese or grab-and-go milk or yogurt.

Above left: Cashew nut 'cheese'; Above: Coconut ice cream

Vegan Desserts

If you love rich and creamy desserts, fear not! Vegan desserts are amazing and much better for your health than dairy-filled ones. Vegan recipes work magic with coconut cream, frozen bananas and even avocados. You will never miss your old favourites. Love custard? Love ice cream? You are in for a vegan treat!

Vegan Baking

Traditional baking calls for copious amounts of eggs, butter and cream. So how does vegan baking work? Cruelty-free baking uses plant-based alternatives and slightly different techniques to create the same effects as traditional baking – whether it's making sure ovens are properly heated, mixing in just the right way or using leavening agents like baking soda or egg substitues such as flax gels. Divine cakes, biscuits, baked desserts and even meringues are possible without causing any harm to animals.

Above: Vegan chocolate banana bread

WHY VEGAN?

ETHICS & ENVIRONMENT

People usually decide to go vegan for ethical reasons. Caring for our fellow animals and the planet, the desire to have no part in the harming of other sentient beings, is a noble and beautiful cause. It's not always an easy decision, but it is an important one.

The Dairy Industry

The mechanized, mass-production dairy industry uses a cruel method of harvesting milk, predominantly from cows, but also from sheep and goats. These gentle mammals produce milk when they give birth, as humans do. The dairy cycle begins with impregnation through artificial insemination. Within 24 hours of being born, calves are removed from their mothers, causing trauma to both. The mother's milk supply is artificially maintained through machine milking, causing more suffering and, often, mastitis infections. One year later, the cycle begins again. A dairy cow is usually considered spent after 7–8 years, instead of their natural 25-year life expectancy, at which point they are slaughtered.

The Fish & Seafood Industry

Overfishing is bringing many species to the brink of extinction, while mercury levels are dangerously high in larger fish. Incidental capture and drowning in fishing nets is the single largest threat to most species of turtles, while an estimated 300,000 small whales, dolphins and porpoises also die this way every year.

The Meat Industry

As well as being cruel, the meat industry is one of the leading causes of deforestation and global warming, due to the feeding of and waste emissions created by billions of farmed animals. Factory farming of animals is incredibly inhumane. They are treated as production units rather than sentient beings, with little or no space to move; feed that contains growth hormones and antibiotics; and short lifespans focused specifically on fattening for slaughter. Even 'free-range' and 'organic' farming methods can be suspect and are not always cruelty-free.

The Egg Industry

From hatching to slaughter, commercial laying hens are mutilated, confined and deprived of their naturally social and curious ways. Even free-range hens may be kept in crowded dark barns at times, and it is common practice to trim the beaks of battery and free-range hens. These laying hens are considered spent after only 12–18

months and sent to slaughter. Then there is the slaughter every year of over 100 million newborn male chicks   no good for the egg industry and the wrong breed for meat.

The Bee Industry

Bees and other pollinators are an essential part of our survival. They pollinate crops to feed us and wild plants to keep the diversity and richness of the planet's flora alive. Consuming bee products in the form of honey, bee pollen, royal jelly, propolis and beeswax exploits these beautiful and important insects.

HEALTH, ENERGY & WELLBEING

Eating a vegan diet often gives people a sense of wellbeing they have not experienced for many years. Eating animal products can be hard on the digestion, as well as acidifying to the body. When you cut these out and eat more whole foods, a natural balance is often restored.

Food Intolerances

Many people have food intolerances they aren't aware of until they cut certain foods out. One of the most common intolerances is to dairy products. Many of us do not produce the enzyme needed to digest dairy, causing mild to severe skin conditions, including:

- Acne and eczema
- Nausea and/or vomiting
- Diarrhoea and/or constipation
- Digestive discomfort
- Runny nose and/or nasal congestion
- Tight chest and difficulty breathing
- Migraines
- Colic in babies

Eggs are another food source that people can be intolerant to, with similar symptoms to those of dairy intolerance. When people become vegan, they often notice a marked improvement in their health.

Weight Loss

Eating a real-food vegan diet can be a healthy way to achieve long-term weight loss. Eating more whole foods means you naturally eat fewer toxic weight-gain foods. A vegan diet is high in fibre, which fills you up and helps with healthy digestion. If you would like to lose weight on a vegan diet, eat a high proportion of fresh vegetables. Stay away from white potatoes, rice and pasta, and eat low-carb vegetables, such as sweet potatoes and plantains instead. Reduce your intake of processed and sweet foods to a minimum and drink plenty of fresh juice and water.

VEGAN SAVINGS

Without the need to buy expensive meat, cheese and fish, having a cruelty-free diet is not just good for the planet, it is good for your wallet too. Real-food veganism is a cost-efficient way to eat, as well as being good for you. Although pre-packaged and processed vegan foods aren't cheap, they tend to be used more as a treat rather than as a staple part of a vegan diet. Vegan cheese and meat substitutes can really hit the spot when you have a craving, but for health and savings, keep your ingredients fresh and real the majority of the time.

A NEW PASSION

Being vegan offers new and exciting avenues for keen cooks. Turning your compassion for the planet into passion in the kitchen will keep you excited and inspired on your vegan journey. There are so many new ways of cooking that become available when you stop relying on standard, animal-based ingredients. Discover what's possible by searching on the internet, buying vegan recipe books, finding local vegan groups and visiting vegan restaurants. Many famous cooks and chefs who used to rely heavily on animal products are now experimenting with plant-based recipes. Your new passion is in fashion!

HUMANITY

Humans are animals, yet this fact is often lost on us. If being vegan is about caring for animals, about not exploiting the animal world, that also includes our own species. Taking care of ourselves and of each other is just as important as taking care of the rest of the animal kingdom. Eat healthily, keep hydrated, get enough sleep and show yourself and your fellow humans kindness and compassion. Try not to preach or judge, and you will be an inspirational vegan. When we take care of ourselves physically and emotionally, we have more love to give every living thing.

MAKING THE TRANSITION

MAKING THE SWITCH

Transitioning to a vegan lifestyle can be a gradual, immediate or partial process. Cutting out animal products is a big adjustment for your body and inevitably leads to potential cravings. Whichever way you make the switch, there are a few points to consider that will make the transition easier, both physically and emotionally.

Gradual Transition

A gradual transition is when you cut one ingredient or animal product out at a time, repeating this over a number of weeks or months until the transition to a vegan

diet is complete. The benefits of a gradual transition include reducing potentially uncomfortable detoxification symptoms, with fewer cravings.

Immediate Transition

An immediate transition is when you exclude animal products all at once. This is the most common way to make the switch – for many, the moral imperative, once acknowledged, becomes very important to fulfil straight away. When all animal products are excluded, people immediately feel in alignment with their beliefs.

A Partial Versus Full Transition

Some vegans feel that the only way to embrace the vegan lifestyle is fully, while others choose to embrace a cruelty-free diet without transitioning their whole lives. Vegan shoes, cosmetics and household products can be expensive and hard to find; you may choose to forego this aspect of the vegan lifestyle.

VEGAN NUTRITION

People often have concerns about how healthy being vegan is. If you don't have these concerns yourself, family and friends may do. While it is possible to be an unhealthy vegan, it is also possible to be vibrantly healthy on a plant-based diet. There are a few common, vegan-related nutritional misconceptions, the main ones being that calcium can only be obtained through dairy products and that meat, fish, eggs and dairy are the only sources of protein. While this is untrue, there are a few key nutrients that it is important to make sure you get enough of.

Protein

Vegan protein sources are abundant, although it is easy not to eat them if you don't know what they are. Plant-based sources of protein that you can enjoy in abundance include nuts and seeds, dark green leafy vegetables, quinoa, buckwheat, seitan, tempeh, soy protein (tofu, TVP) and rice combined with beans.

Vitamin B12

As a vegan, you cannot get adequate amounts of B12 through your diet. It is essential to supplement with B12 patches, a sublingual spray and/or consistent consumption of foods fortified with B12. Have your B12 levels tested regularly to make sure you are not deficient in this essential vitamin.

Calcium

Getting enough calcium on a vegan diet is actually surprisingly easy. Sources include kale, rocket (arugula), broccoli, swede (rutabaga), parsley, oranges, nuts and seeds. Historically, spinach was thought to be a good source of calcium, but we now know that this isn't true – it contains oxalate, which hinders the absorption of its calcium.

Vitamin D

Vitamin D teams up with calcium for strong, healthy bones. While much of our vitamin D comes through skin exposure to the sun, most people do not get enough sunlight for adequate vitamin D absorption. As the main dietary source for this important vitamin is fatty fish, vegans are particularly susceptible to deficiency, so may need to take supplements. Make sure they are vegan, as many are not.

Iron

Getting enough iron means eating plenty of wholefoods. Plant-based sources of iron include dried fruits, dark green leafy vegetables, seeds, pulses, potatoes and whole grains. Vitamin C is needed to maximize iron absorption, so combine these ingredients with vitamin C-rich foods, such as oranges, blackcurrants, broccoli, mango and parsley.

Good Fats

Omega-3 and omega-6 fats are essential for healthy cell function, energy and overall wellbeing. While our modern diets contain plenty of omega-6, omega-3 is harder to come by. For great health, focus on eating plenty of foods rich in omega-3, including ground flaxseed and chia seeds, spirulina, walnuts and hemp.

VEGAN PARENTING

As a vegan parent, it is only natural that you might want to bring your children up vegan too. There are some important health aspects to take into consideration when bringing kids up on a plant-based diet, as potential nutritional deficiencies in children are impactful on brain development and growth.

Transitioning Kids to Cruelty-free Living

While research strongly supports vegan nutrition for children, infants and babies, it is highly recommended that you research potential nutritional deficiencies and make a plan for counteracting these with whole foods, supplements and fortified foods. There are excellent websites and blogs dedicated to vegan parenting that will help you.

Vegan Pregnancy

Many thousands of healthy babies are born to vegan mothers every year. As with all expectant mothers, it is important for the vegan mum-to-be to get adequate nutrition and hydration during her pregnancy. The Vegan Society provides a free downloadable booklet to help navigate nutrition for a plant-based pregnancy and nursing.

Vegan Nursing

As a breastfeeding mother, if you are nutritionally deficient, your baby will be too. Deficiency can affect your child's development and overall health, so research which nutrients are essential while nursing. There is at present no vegan infant formula available. Commercial plant-based formulas are fortified with vitamins from animal sources.

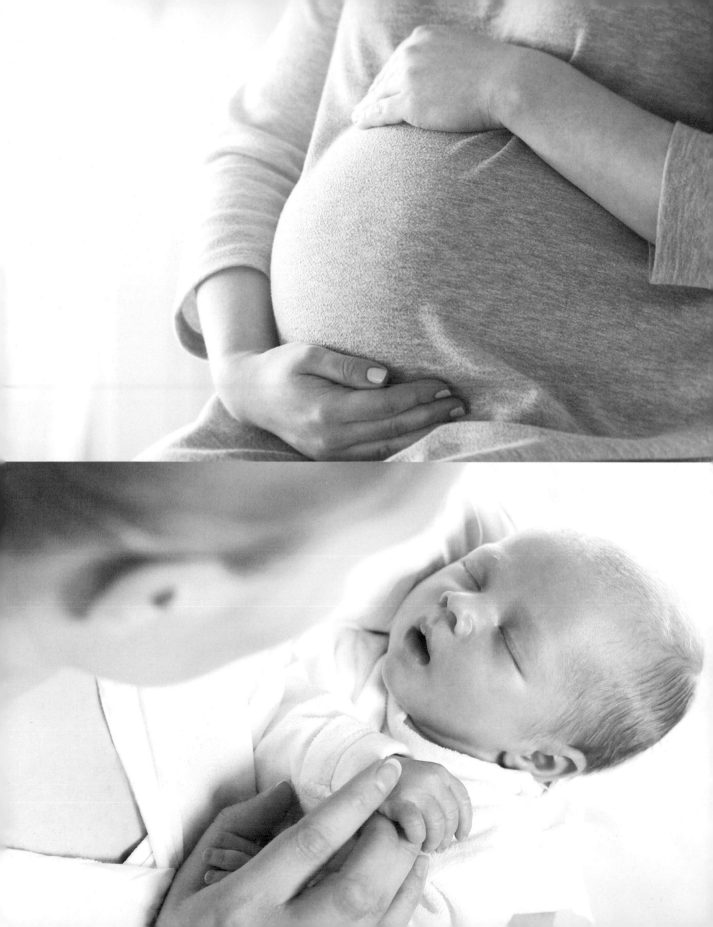

KEY VEGAN FOODS

FRESH INGREDIENTS

Fresh produce should be the staple element of a healthy vegan diet. Fruits and vegetables will give you energy as well as helping you maintain a healthy weight. This is where many of your essential nutrients come from. Eat a rainbow of colours for a broad spectrum of vitamins and minerals.

Herbs & Spices

Fresh herbs and spices introduce the potential for exotic and international flavours to be created simply and quickly. Have you tried fresh Thai curry paste, made with fresh ginger, garlic, chili (pepper), coriander (cilantro) and lime? It is out of this world! Or an Italian bake with fresh oregano (*see* page 196)? Just you wait!

Vegetables

Vegetables come in all shapes and sizes. They can be eaten raw, lightly cooked, stewed or baked. There is so much creativity at your fingertips through this deliciously earth-bound food source! Whether you grow your own, buy from farmers' markets or the superstore, make veggies a major part of your vegan diet. From roots and tubers, to leaves, to veggie fruits; from brassicas to alliums to fungi; the variety available to us today is breathtaking. Their amazing flavours, textures and colours provide us with life-giving nutrients.

Fruit

Fruit is a major source of healthy carbohydrate. It is hydrating, full of vitamins and incredibly diverse in its uses. On a vegan diet, you can enjoy it as a light breakfast, added to cooked porridge (oatmeal), served in savoury salads, and in a wide range of desserts. It is important to eat a range of fruit – each colour represents a different nutritional component, and we need a wide spectrum of vitamins and minerals for optimum mental and physical health. If you want to, stick to low glycaemic fruits, such as fresh berries, citrus and orchard fruit like apples and nectarines.

STORECUPBOARD INGREDIENTS

As a vegan cook, you will be happiest when your cupboards are stocked with dried goods and bottled ingredients, allowing you to create something delicious, even when you are out of fresh produce. You will use these ingredients in everything, from savoury and sweet breakfasts, to light lunches and hearty evening meals.

Nuts & Seeds

Nuts and seeds are a great source of protein. They are also a fantastic source of essential healthy fats. You can make delicious vegan milks and cheese substitutes with them, as well as adding nuts and seeds to your breakfasts, smoothies, and sweet and savoury recipes for added texture and flavour.

Beans, Pulses & Legumes

Beans, pulses and legumes are a staple part of most vegan diets. They bring a satisfying texture and flavour to any dish, and can be whizzed up into dips and soups to make a filling light meal. Beans, pulses and legumes include lentils, chickpeas, kidney beans, butter (lima) beans, soya beans, haricot beans, black beans, cannellini beans, split peas and mung beans. Most beans and pulses need to be pre-soaked before cooking. Lentils are an exception to this rule and can be cooked without soaking. They are often a favourite for their flavour and speed of cooking, compared with other dried beans.

Herbs, Spices & Condiments

Investing in staple dried herbs and spices will open up a wide range of vegan recipes. Popular herbs in vegan cooking include oregano, thyme, bay leaves, sage, parsley and Italian mixed herbs. Spices for vegan dishes include curry powders, ground cumin, ground coriander, smoked paprika, turmeric, mustard seeds, pepper, good-quality mineral salt, cinnamon, nutmeg, vanilla extract and cardamom. With vegan condiments you can bring depth and added flavour to your recipes. Favourites include soy sauce and tamari, mustard, nutritional yeast flakes, sun-dried tomato paste, vegetable bouillon, hot chili sauce, barbecue sauce, ketchup, vegan mayonnaise and vegan Worcestershire sauce.

Oils

Most plant-derived oils are highly processed and toxic to the body when cooked. Healthy oils include extra-virgin coconut and olive oils. Other cold-pressed oils

that are super good for vegans when used raw, delicious in salad dressings and drizzled straight over cooked food, include hemp oil, flaxseed oil and avocado oil.

Vinegars

Vinegar is vegan and there is a wide range of delicious options available. Use vinegar in salad dressings, in marinades for vegetables, tofu and tempeh, and to flavour dishes. Favourite types of vinegar include balsamic vinegar, red or white wine vinegar and apple cider vinegar.

Vegan Sweeteners

Apart from honey, most sweeteners are vegan, but many are not good for you and their mass production causes harm to our planet. There are many healthy, plant-based sweeteners that have a lesser impact on the environment and can be

Above: Stevia granules; Above right: Date syrup

easily used in baking, in desserts and as a condiment. Avoid artificial sweeteners completely. More and more research is coming to light about the damaging effects of artificial sweeteners on our long-term health. Favourite healthy vegan sweeteners include coconut sugar, maple syrup, date syrup and stevia. Try to use them when possible if you want to be a healthy vegan.

Grains

Grains are another staple in the vegan diet. Although they contain many essential nutrients, it is easy to overeat grains, particularly wheat. Many people are intolerant to wheat without realizing, so keep it to a minimum and, if you can, find products using older strains of wheat – such as spelt, which has been found to be more easily digested by many people. Your body will thank you for it!

Other delicious grains that work beautifully on a vegan diet include oats, rice, quinoa, millet, amaranth, barley and corn. Cook them in their whole form to use in savoury dishes, or use the rolled versions in breakfast porridge (oatmeal), muesli and granola.

VEGAN ALTERNATIVES

Dairy Substitutes

There are vegan substitutes for milk, butter, cheese and yogurt available in most superstores and health food stores. Milk substitutes usually come as tetra-packed, plant-based milks such as rice milk, oat milk, soya milk, almond milk and coconut milk. Try them out to see which one works for you. Vegan margarine-like spreads are made from emulsified plant oils and other ingredients. With pre-packaged cheese substitutes, be aware that some brands are better than others for that melted-cheese effect. Vegan yogurt is usually made from soy or coconut milk. See the 'Staples' section on page 70 for how to make your own delicious dairy alternatives.

Egg Substitutes

You can buy vegan 'egg-replacer' for use in baking and desserts, or you can make your own. To replace one egg:

1 tablespoon ground flaxseed
3 tablespoons water

Combine the ground flaxseed and water, and use when required. Adjust the recipe proportionately according to the number of eggs needed.

Meat Substitutes

These days, there are vegan substitutes for most flavours of meat, from bacon to sausages, burgers to chicken. More generic meat substitutes include TVP (textured vegetable protein), made from soy; tempeh, made from fermented whole soya beans; and seitan, which is made from wheat flour – all of which you can flavour yourself. Another meat substitute you may be aware of is the 'mycoprotein'-based Quorn – unfortunately, many of Quorn's products are not vegan as they contain egg, though they do now have a vegan range.

PRE-PACKAGED FOODS

There is a huge selection of pre-packaged vegan foods available. Veganism has become more mainstream and the food industry has stepped up to provide for this niche. Pre-packaged vegan foods range from the dairy, meat and milk substitutes already mentioned to ingredients such as tofu, vegan mayonnaise, dips, ready-prepared meals, vegan ice cream, desserts, chocolate and sweets (candy). This is part of the reason it is easy to be a 'junk' vegan. Although it costs more, the convenience is undeniable. As long as the focus is on a balanced, mainly wholefood vegan diet, enjoy your favourite pre-packaged foods guilt-free.

Top: Ground flaxseed to make egg substitute; Bottom: Soy meatballs

FOODS TO AVOID

It is not always obvious which foods contain animal products. Here are some foods that may catch you out:

- Gelatine, made from the connective tissue of pigs and cows – used in many sweets (candies), as well as in jelly (jello).
- Refined sugar can be lightened with bone char, derived from the bones of cattle.
- Certain food additives, including E120, E322, E422, E471, E542, E631, E901 and E904, are sometimes derived from animals.
- Cochineal, or carmine, red food colouring is made from insects.
- Isinglass, from fish bladders, is often used in beer and wine-making.
- Products enriched with omega-3 and vitamin D3 usually use animal sources for these nutrients.
- Shellac, an insect-based product, is sometimes used to wax fresh produce or glaze sweets (candies).
- Whey, casein and lactose, common additives in many pre-packaged foods, are all derived from dairy.
- Some bread products contain L-cysteine, which often comes from feathers, to keep them soft.
- Olive tapenade often contains anchovies, as do some condiments and ready-made sauces.
- The batter on deep-fried foods often contains eggs.
- Pasta, especially fresh pasta, often contains eggs.

As a rule, look for brands or products that are marked 'cruelty-free' or 'vegan' and read the ingredients labels on other foods to make sure that they don't contain animal products.

TOOLS & EQUIPMENT

KiTCHEN KiT

You don't need any particular kit as a vegan cook, but knowing what you are going to use to make your new vegan recipes will help you feel creative and confident in the kitchen. Plus, you might want to add to what you already have in order to expand the possibilities.

Cooking Pots & Pans

STEAMER

A single or double steamer pan is used for lightly cooking vegetables so that they retain their nutrients, rather than losing them in boiling water.

PRESSURE COOKER

A pan with a pressurized lid that is great for speeding up the cooking time of pulses and stews.

STOCKPOT

A large, deep pan for making soups and stocks, as well as for cooking larger quantities of food.

FRYING PAN

Used for frying and sautéing anything from vegetables to vegan burgers to caramelized pineapple and pancakes.

ROASTING PANS

For baking and roasting in the oven.

GRIDDLE

For that lovely barbecue flavour straight off the grill, but on your hob (stove) instead. Great for griddling sliced vegetables, seitan and vegan burgers.

NONSTICK PANS

For making sweet and savoury sauces, and for cooking rice and pasta.

MILK PAN

For cooking small quantities of food and for heating up vegan milks.

Slicing & Dicing

Good knives are a cook's best friend. They make the preparation of food easy and safe. The sharper your knives are, the safer your fingers are.

LARGE KITCHEN KNIFE

One with a curved blade is a good all-round chopping utensil. Use it to slice harder fruits and vegetables, and to chop herbs.

PARING KNIFE

This is great for cutting smaller and softer fruits and vegetables, as well as for peeling.

BREAD KNIFE

A good bread knife makes life a lot easier if you are a fan of rustic or homemade breads.

VEGETABLE PEELER & GRATER

These are essential for any keen cook.

Processing

A food processor is a very handy piece of kitchen equipment for the vegan cook to own. It comes with a selection of blades that make chopping, dicing and slicing fast, efficient and fun. It can be used to make burger mixes, dips, salsas, sauces, dressings, toppings for baked savouries, biscuits, desserts, cake batters and much more – all in a matter of minutes.

Blending

Blenders come in a range of prices, speeds and qualities. With even a cheap handheld blender, you will be able to expand your recipe repertoire to include smoothies, soups, sweet and savoury sauces, dips, dressings, dairy-free milks, homemade vegan baby foods and more. With a good-quality, high-speed blender, you can really create magic. Vegan ice cream, mousses and vegan cheesecake mixes become possible with the push of a button. Pancake batter can be made in moments, ready for that weekend breakfast, and in five minutes you can whip up a banana sundae to be enjoyed in front of an evening movie.

Dairy-free Milk Maker

It is very easy to make your own dairy-free milks. The low-tech version is simply to use a muslin cloth (cheesecloth) and bowl – just blend your ingredients before straining your milk through the cloth. If you prefer something less labour intensive and more efficient, you can buy a dairy-free milk maker. There is a cold setting for making raw milks, such as almond or sesame milk, and a hot setting for making cooked milks, such as soya milk, rice milk or oat milk.

PREPARATION & TECHNIQUES

FOOD SAFETY & HYGIENE

Food poisoning from vegan food is rare as it contains no animal products, the usual suspect in food poisoning. It is, however, recommended that you always wash fresh fruits and vegetables as they can carry bacteria that may upset your stomach. In your refrigerator, keep different types of ingredients on different shelves. If some of your household eat meat or dairy, keep it in sealed containers, and have a chopping (cutting) board specifically for meat. Having separate chopping boards for fruits and vegetables will avoid cross-contamination. Eat pre-packaged food by the use-by date and, once opened, within the time frame specified.

VEGAN COOKING

Most vegan cooking techniques are the same as standard techniques, with a few exceptions. Vegan cakes are made in a different way to standard cakes because we cannot use the alchemy of the butter/sugar/egg combination. Vegan dishes do not use eggs as a setting agent, which calls for different approaches.

Steaming

Steaming is a simple technique using the heat of steam to cook vegetables and fruit. Ingredients are suspended above boiling water using a steaming pan, or a collapsible steamer basket inside a normal saucepan. Steaming, as opposed to boiling, retains more of the nutrients, with less goodness leaching into the water.

Sautéing

Sautéing is the term used for light frying. Slice your vegetables finely. Place a small amount of oil or water (known as 'water frying') in the bottom of your frying pan. Once the oil or water is hot, add the finely sliced vegetables and cook, stirring, until just tender.

Roasting & Baking

Roasting and baking is when you cook something in the oven. The most important factor to remember when roasting or baking is to turn on your oven to the required temperature 15 minutes before you start cooking, in order to bring it up to temperature. This is particularly important when baking.

Boiling

Boiling is most useful for cooking grains and starches such as rice, quinoa, pasta, oats and potatoes. Simply add the required amount of water to a saucepan, bring the water to the boil with a little salt and/or oil, and add your ingredient. Reduce the heat and simmer until cooked.

Slow Cooking

Cooking ingredients for many hours is generally not considered healthy, as so many nutrients are destroyed with long cooking times. However, slow cooking soups and stews for 1½–6 hours leaches the goodness out of the ingredients into the broth, creating melt-in-the-mouth recipes while retaining many of the nutrients.

Grilling & Griddling

To grill (broil), place patties, burgers or vegetables under a medium-hot grill (broiler) until browned. Do the same for melted vegan cheese toppings. To use a griddle pan, preheat until hot. Brush the burgers, patties or thin slices of vegetables with oil and cook for 5–7 minutes on each side.

Pressure Cooking

Pressure cooking, which uses a specialized pressure cooker, is used as a fast way to cook beans and pulses. Refer to your pressure cooker manual for how to cook specific pulses in your brand of cooker. Take extra care when releasing the pressure from the pot at the end of cooking.

CONVERTING RECIPES

Converting a traditional recipe into a vegan version is a fun and creative process. The simplest way to find recipes for favourite dishes is to do an internet search with 'vegan' in the search bar, for example 'vegan lasagne' or 'vegan carrot cake'.
If you want to try converting a recipe yourself, here are some easy tips for substitutions:

• Use TVP, tofu or some other vegan meat replacement instead of meat
• Use vegan cheese instead of dairy cheese
• Use vegan egg replacer or flax egg (*see* page 53) instead of poultry eggs
• Use dairy-free milk instead of dairy milk
• Use maple syrup instead of honey.

STAPLES

VEGAN MAYONNAISE

Vegan mayonnaise is easier to make than traditional mayonnaise. Just throw it all in the blender and you are good to go! For added excitement add garlic, fresh herbs or spices.

Makes about 250 ml/ 8 fl oz/ 1 cup

225 g/8 oz silken tofu, drained
2 tbsp light olive oil
1 tbsp lemon juice
½ tsp salt
1 tsp Dijon mustard

Blend all the ingredients in a blender until smooth and creamy. Store in the refrigerator for up to a week.

PLANT-BASED BUTTERY SPREAD

It is always nice to have something buttery to spread on your toast or put on hot jacket potatoes. Many of the vegan butter alternatives aren't that good for you, but this one is, and it tastes divine too.

Makes 200 ml/7 fl oz/ scant 1 cup

125 g/4 oz/½ cup coconut oil
50 ml/2 fl oz/¼ cup light olive oil
pinch salt
2 tbsp macadamia nuts or pine nuts

Melt the coconut oil in a pan over a low heat. Once melted, add to a blender with the remaining ingredients and blend until smooth.

Transfer to a sterilized jar and store in the refrigerator for up to a month.

ALMOND, OAT & RICE MILKS

Dairy-free milks are easy to make and freeze well. They last 1–2 days in the refrigerator, so make them fresh or freeze in small batches.

Makes 750 ml/1¼ pints/3 cups

For the oat milk

75 g/3 oz/¾ cup rolled oats
750 ml/1¼ pints/3 cups water

For the raw almond milk

225 g/8 oz/1½ cups whole almonds,
    soaked overnight and rinsed
750 ml/1¼ pints/3 cups water

For the rice milk

150 g/5 oz/scant 1 cup cooked brown rice
750 ml/1¼ pints/3 cups water

For the optional flavouring

1–2 tsp maple syrup
½ tsp vanilla extract

Blend your chosen milk ingredients in a blender until smooth and creamy.

For the first strain, pour the mixture into a sieve (strainer), and use a spoon to scrape the bottom of the sieve to keep the milk straining through.

If you like your milk silky smooth, strain again using a nut milk bag, fine cloth or clean tea (dish) towel. Line a large bowl or jug with the cloth and pour the mixture into the cloth. Pull up the edges of the cloth and hold them in your hand, so that the mixture strains into the bowl. Use your other hand to squeeze the mixture through the cloth.

CUSTARD

Custard is such a delicious and comforting sauce, but how do you make it without eggs or milk? Try this version with slices of banana or poured over baked desserts.

Serves 1 as a dessert or 3 as a sauce

300 ml/10 fl oz/1¼ cups unsweetened almond, rice or oat milk (*see* page 76)

1 tbsp cornflour (cornstarch)

1 tsp vanilla extract

50 g/2 oz/¼ cup sugar

pinch salt

pinch ground turmeric (optional)

Set 3 tablespoons milk aside. Heat the remaining milk in a pan until just before boiling.

Place the remaining ingredients with 1 tablespoon of the reserved milk in a heatproof bowl and mix thoroughly. Add another tablespoon of milk and mix thoroughly, making sure there are no lumps, before adding the final tablespoon.

Slowly pour the hot milk over the ingredients, stirring, then return the mixture to the pan and bring to the boil, stirring constantly to stop it sticking. Serve.

COCONUT YOGURT

This yummy, dairy-free yogurt is great for breakfast or as a topping for desserts. You can get acidophilus probiotic from any good health food store.

Serves 2

400 ml/14 fl oz can coconut milk
4 capsules acidophilus probiotic
½ tsp xanthan gum

Preheat a thermos flask.

Heat the milk in a very clean pan until just warm (do not overheat – you want it to be just warm to the touch), then pour into a blender with the acidophilus and xanthan gum and blend until smooth.

Pour the mixture into the preheated flask and leave for 12 hours. After 12 hours, the yogurt is ready. Pour into sterilized jars. Chill for up to 10 days.

Note

To make a large batch, adjust the recipe proprtionately and pour the mixture into sterilized glass jars in the oven, with just the light on, for 12 hours. The heat from the light is enough to culture the yogurt.

VANILLA ICE CREAM

This is the simplest, easiest and quickest ice cream to make, and it tastes amazing! Kids and adults will love this sweet dairy-free treat.

Serves 2

4 frozen bananas

2 tsp vanilla extract

3 tbsp water

Using a blender, blitz all the ingredients until smooth. Eat immediately or freeze for later. If you freeze it, remove from the freezer 10 minutes before serving to soften. Store in the freezer for up to a month.

Variations

Simply add a different choice of frozen fruit and/or flavouring when blending.

Note

To prepare frozen bananas, peel ripe bananas and cut into large slices before freezing.

BREAKFAST & BRUNCH

BREAKFAST PANCAKES

Pancakes are the ultimate weekend treat. Here they are topped with berries and coconut, but you could use banana and maple syrup or Chocolate Hazelnut Spread (*see* page 204).

Makes 8 pancakes

For the pancakes

200 g/7 oz/1½ cups plain (all-purpose) flour

1 tbsp ground flaxseed

2 tsp baking powder

¼ tsp salt

1 tsp unrefined granulated sugar or maple syrup

300 ml/10 fl oz/1¼ cups unsweetened dairy-free milk

1 tsp vanilla extract

coconut oil, for cooking

For the topping

4 tbsp strawberry or raspberry jam

1 handful desiccated (dry unsweetened) coconut

2 tbsp water

2 handfuls blueberries

2 handfuls strawberries, halved

For the topping, heat the jam, coconut and water in a small pan, stirring to combine, then set aside. Preheat the oven to its lowest temperature. Blend all the pancake ingredients, except the oil, until smooth. Heat a little oil in a frying pan over a medium-high heat. Ladle 4 tablespoons of batter at a time into the pan, allowing each pancake to spread naturally. Cook for 3 minutes on each side until lightly browned. Once cooked, keep warm in the oven while you cook the next batch. Top with the sauce and fruit.

FRENCH TOAST

French toast is such a luxurious breakfast! Here it's topped with blueberries, but it's also delicious topped with slices of banana or mango.

Serves 2

125 ml/4 fl oz/½ cup unsweetened dairy-free milk

3 tbsp plain (all-purpose) flour

1 tbsp maple syrup, plus extra for drizzling

½ tsp ground cinnamon

½ tsp vanilla extract

4 thick slices bread

coconut oil, for frying

1 handful blueberries

icing (confectioners') sugar (optional)

Whisk the milk, flour, maple syrup, cinnamon and vanilla together, then pour the mixture into a wide shallow dish. Quickly dip both sides of the bread into the batter – don't let the slices get too soggy.

Heat 2 tablespoons oil in a frying pan over a medium-high heat and cook the French toast for 3 minutes on each side until golden brown. Add more oil, if necessary. Serve drizzled with maple syrup and topped with blueberries. Dust with icing (confectioners') sugar, if liked.

QUINOA PORRIDGE WITH BERRIES

Quinoa is amazingly good for you and one of the best sources of plant protein. Although it is mostly used in savoury dishes, it is delicious for breakfast.

Serves 1

250 ml/8 fl oz/1 cup unsweetened dairy-free milk

pinch salt (optional)

½ tsp vanilla extract

1 tbsp unrefined granulated sugar or maple syrup

40 g/1½ oz/scant ½ cup quinoa flakes

1 handful frozen berries

1 handful fresh blueberries

mint leaves (optional)

Combine the milk, salt (if using), vanilla and sugar in a pan. Bring to the boil, stirring. Once the milk is boiling, stir in the quinoa. Turn off the heat and leave for 3 minutes until soft and creamy. Pour into a bowl and top with berries and mint, if liked.

OVERNIGHT BREAKFAST POT

This beautiful breakfast is jam-packed with superfood goodness to get your day off to a brilliant start. Prepare the base the night before, and add the fruit in the morning.

Serves 1

50 g/2 oz/½ cup rolled oats

1 tbsp chia seeds

1 handful goji berries

300 ml/10 fl oz/1¼ cups unsweetened almond milk

fresh fruit of choice, such as apricots or nectarines

Mix the oats, chia seeds, goji berries and milk together and pour into a glass jar or bowl. Chill overnight.

The next morning, stir the oat mixture and top with fruit.

BREAKFAST TACOS

A simple weekend brunch. When buying spiced canned beans, check they are vegan. Bought salsa verde usually contains anchovies, and homemade tastes so much better!

Serves 1

2 small flour tortillas

200 g/7 oz/1¼ cups canned spicy mixed beans

½ ripe avocado, sliced

50 g/2 oz/½ cup grated vegan cheese

For the salsa verde

½ garlic clove, peeled and very finely chopped

2 tsp capers

2 tbsp finely chopped parsley

2 tbsp finely chopped basil

2 tbsp finely chopped mint

½ tsp Dijon mustard

2 tsp white wine vinegar

1 tbsp olive oil

freshly ground black pepper

Mix all the salsa ingredients together in a bowl and leave to stand. Lightly heat the tortillas in a frying pan. Serve topped with the mixed beans, avocado, grated cheese and salsa verde.

Tip

If you are doing a taco brunch, wrap all the tortillas in foil and put them in the oven preheated to 150°C/300°F/Gas Mark 2 for 20 minutes before serving.

CHOCO BANANA OATMEAL

Banana and chocolate for breakfast? You bet! Combined with oats, this makes the perfect early morning treat.

Serves 2

500 ml/18 fl oz/2 cups water

150 g/5 oz/1½ cups quick porridge oats

3 tbsp unsweetened cocoa powder

1 tsp vanilla extract

3 tbsp unrefined granulated sugar or other vegan sweetener

pinch salt

To serve

1 banana, peeled and sliced

vegan yogurt (optional)

1 handful chopped untoasted cashew nuts (optional)

Bring all the ingredients to the boil in a pan, stirring. Reduce the heat and simmer for 10 minutes, stirring occasionally. If it starts to get too thick, add a little water.

Serve topped with banana. Add yogurt and cashews, if liked.

BERRY POWER SMOOTHIE BOWL

This bowl is packed full of all the goodness of a smoothie, with the added bonus of being more substantial, to fill you up.

Serves 1

For the smoothie

65 ml/2½ fl oz/generous ¼ cup water

4 handfuls frozen mixed berries

1 ripe banana, peeled

½ tsp acai powder (optional)

To serve

1 small handful sliced toasted almonds

1 small handful fresh berries, such as blackberries and blueberries

1 banana, peeled and sliced

1 tbsp pumpkin seeds

½ tbsp chia seeds

Put all the smoothie ingredients in a blender and blend until smooth. Pour into a bowl and serve, topped with almonds, fruit and seeds.

PAPRIKA TOMATOES ON TOAST

There is so much scope for delicious savoury vegan breakfasts. This richly satisfying spread is great on any kind of toast. Try it on rice cakes or oatcakes for a lighter alternative.

Serves 2

1 tbsp olive oil

1 spring onion (scallion), chopped

2 tomatoes, chopped

1 tbsp dried oregano

¼ tsp smoked paprika

pinch unrefined granulated sugar

¼ tsp unrefined salt

4 sun-dried tomato halves, in oil or rehydrated, chopped

1 thick slice white or brown bread, chopped

3 tbsp toasted almonds

freshly ground black pepper

4 slices toast

flat-leaf parsley, to garnish (optional)

Heat the oil in a frying pan over a medium-low heat and fry the spring onions (scallions) for 5 minutes until soft. Add the chopped tomatoes, oregano, paprika, sugar and salt, increase the heat to medium and simmer for 5 minutes. Transfer to a food processor, add the sun-dried tomatoes, bread, almonds and pepper and blitz until well combined but still with texture.

Serve on toast, topped with parsley, if liked.

SMOOTHiES & DRiNKS

CREAMY BANANA OAT SMOOTHIE

This smoothie makes a delicious breakfast or mid-morning snack. It's filling and light at the same time, and the vanilla gives it a luxurious quality that everyone loves.

Makes 1 large or 2 smaller glasses

300 ml/10 fl oz/1¼ cups unsweetened almond or coconut milk

6 ice cubes

2 ripe bananas, peeled

1 large handful rolled oats

½ tsp vanilla extract

1 tsp ground cinnamon

Blend all the ingredients together until smooth and creamy. Serve.

GREEN ENERGY YOGURT SMOOTHIE

Yogurt smoothies are a delicious cross between a drink and a meal. If you have never had a green smoothie before, this is the perfect introduction to these energy-giving elixirs.

Makes 1 large or 2 smaller glasses

300 ml/10 fl oz/1¼ cups vegan yogurt

15 g/½ oz/½ cup kale leaves, without stalks

1 tbsp maple syrup, plus extra to taste (optional)

Blend all the ingredients together until smooth and creamy. Add more maple syrup if you prefer it sweeter.

TROPICAL SMOOTHIE

When you want some sunshine, go for this smoothie. It is the essence of the tropics in a glass!

Makes 1 large or 2 smaller glasses

75 g/3 oz/½ cup fresh or frozen pineapple chunks

75 g/3 oz/½ cup fresh or frozen mango chunks

1 ripe banana, peeled

300 ml/10 fl oz/1¼ cups coconut water

4 ice cubes

mild chili powder, for sprinkling (optional)

Blend the fruit, coconut water and ice together in a blender until smooth and creamy. Serve cold with a sprinkling of chili powder on top if you like it spicy.

PINK LEMONADE

The colour of this refreshing drink is gorgeous. The combination of lemon and pink grapefruit are magic and, despite the adult flavours, kids love it too. For fresh grapefruit juice, squeeze 3–4 pink grapefruits.

Makes 2 litres / 3½ pints / 8 cups

300 g/11 oz/1⅔ cups unrefined granulated sugar
1 litre/1¾ pints/4 cups water
5 lemons
750 ml/1¼ pints/3 cups pink grapefruit juice
ice cubes, to serve

Put the sugar and 250 ml/8 fl oz/1 cup water in a small pan over a low heat, stirring to dissolve the sugar. Once the sugar has dissolved, chill in the refrigerator or freezer to cool.

Juice the lemons and grapefruits (if using fresh grapefruit), straining out the pulp. Combine the remaining water with the fruit juices and sugar syrup in a jug (pitcher). Serve with ice. Chill for up to 2 days.

MINT CUCUMBER COOLER

When the weather is hot and you need a cooling pick-me-up, this drink is perfect.

Makes 1 litre/1¾ pints/4 cups

1 tbsp maple syrup or other vegan sweetener

1 litre/1¾ pints/4 cups water

1 handful mint leaves, plus extra to garnish

¼ cucumber, thinly sliced

ice cubes, to serve

Place the maple syrup and water in a jug and stir until dissolved. Bruise the mint leaves by rubbing them between your fingers, then add to the water and chill for a few hours.

Once the water has infused with mint, strain and add the cucumber. Serve with ice and fresh mint leaves. Chill for up to 48 hours.

STRAWBERRY MILKSHAKE

Balsamic vinegar may seem like a strange ingredient to add to strawberry milkshake, but it creates a special alchemy that brings out the flavour of the strawberries. Freeze the coconut milk in an ice tray in advance.

Makes 1 large or 2 smaller glasses

300 g/11 oz/1½ cups frozen strawberries

125 ml/4 fl oz/½ cup frozen full-fat canned coconut milk

1–2 tbsp maple syrup or other vegan sweetener

½ tsp balsamic vinegar (optional)

few fresh strawberries, for topping

Blend all the ingredients until thoroughly combined. Spoon into tall glasses and top with fresh strawberries.

MINT CHOCOLATE MILKSHAKE

Chocolate and mint is such a classic combination, and this drinkable variation is luxury in a glass. Treat yourself!

Makes 1 large or 2 smaller glasses

250 ml/8 fl oz/1 cup unsweetened almond or soya milk

50 ml/2 fl oz/¼ cup almond or soy cream

4 ice cubes

1 ripe banana, peeled

2 drops organic mint essential oil

2 tbsp unsweetened cocoa powder

pinch salt

1–2 tsp unrefined granulated sugar or maple syrup (optional)

For the toppings (optional)

grated vegan chocolate

fresh mint leaves

Blend all the milkshake ingredients until smooth. Add toppings, if liked, and serve cold.

CINNAMON HOT CHOCOLATE

Canned coconut milk is much creamier than coconut milk from a carton, so it makes this drink comforting for a cold evening or mid-morning break.

Makes 1 mug

150 ml/¼ pint/⅔ cup canned full-fat coconut milk

150 ml/¼ pint/⅔ cup water

1 tsp ground cinnamon

½ tsp vanilla extract

pinch salt

1 tbsp unsweetened cocoa powder

1 tbsp maple syrup or other vegan sweetener

Gently heat the milk, water, cinnamon, vanilla and salt in a small pan until just before boiling. Mix the cocoa and sweetener in a mug with 1 tablespoon of the hot milk mixture. Stir until smooth, then add the remaining milk.

DIPS, SAUCES & SNACKS

BLACK BEAN & PUMPKIN SEED DIP

This is a Mexican take on hummus. It has a lovely, almost purple colour and the full flavour of the black beans marries beautifully with the lime and coriander (cilantro).

Serves 2-4

200 g/7 oz/ scant 1¼ cups canned black beans

1 handful coriander (cilantro) leaves

2 handfuls toasted pumpkin seeds

1 tbsp lime juice

2 tbsp olive oil

2 tbsp water

1 garlic clove, peeled and crushed

¼ tsp salt

bread or tortilla chips, to serve

Set aside a few black beans and some coriander (cilantro).

Blitz the rest of the ingredients in a food processor well, but leave some texture. Spoon into a bowl, garnish with the reserved black beans and coriander and serve with bread or tortillas.

DAIRY-FREE TZATZIKI

The Greeks have many delicious vegetarian recipes, many of them vegan too. And if they aren't traditionally vegan, it's easy to adapt them.

Serves 4 as a dip or side dish

1 cucumber, peeled and coarsely grated

1 tsp salt

300 g/11 oz/1¼ cups vegan yogurt

2 garlic cloves, peeled and crushed

2 tbsp olive oil

2 tsp lemon juice

1 tsp chopped mint

1 tsp chopped dill

freshly ground black pepper

crusty bread or crudités, to serve

Place the cucumber in a sieve (strainer) set over a bowl and sprinkle with ½ teaspoon of the salt. Leave to stand.

Mix the remaining salt with the yogurt, garlic, oil, lemon juice and chopped herbs.

Using your hand or the back of a spoon, squeeze the grated cucumber against the sides of the sieve (strainer) to remove as much cucumber juice as possible. Stir the squeezed cucumber through the yogurt mix. Season with pepper and chill for a few hours. Serve as a dip with crusty bread or crudités. Chill for up to 48 hours.

BARBECUE SAUCE

The sweet and savoury spiciness of barbecue sauce is delicious with lots of vegan recipes. Try it with fries, burgers, seitan, lunch wraps and as a dip.

Makes 1 litre/1³/₄ pints/4 cups

220 g/7¾ oz/1½ cups brown sugar

360 g/12½ oz/1½ cups tomato ketchup

125 ml/4 fl oz/½ cup red wine vinegar

125 ml/4 fl oz/½ cup water

1 tbsp vegan Worcestershire sauce

2½ tbsp English (yellow) mustard

2 garlic cloves

2 tsp smoked paprika

1 tsp ground ginger

1 tsp ground cinnamon

¼ tsp ground nutmeg

2 tsp salt

1½ tsp black pepper

2 dashes hot chili sauce (optional)

Put all the ingredients into a small saucepan and slowly bring to the boil. Reduce the heat and simmer for 5 minutes. Cool before decanting into a sterilized glass bottle or jar. Chill for up to a month.

CHEEZE SAUCE

This dairy-free cheeze sauce is so simple to make. Pour it over steamed vegetables and rice, stir it through pasta or serve it as a hot dip with Rainbow Oven Fries (*see* page 138).

Makes 300 ml/½ pint/1¼ cups

250 ml/8 fl oz/1 cup water

130 g/4½ oz/1 cup cashew nuts

1 tbsp lemon juice

2 spring onions (scallions), chopped

2 tbsp nutritional yeast flakes

¾ tsp salt

Blend all the ingredients together until smooth, then gently heat in a pan until thick and creamy.

RAINBOW OVEN FRIES

Fries are such a comforting snack or side dish. Mix up your root veggies for a colour and taste sensation!

Makes 1 big plate of fries

2 potatoes, peeled

1 large beetroot, peeled

1 sweet potato, peeled

1 carrot, peeled

1 large parsnip, peeled

3 tbsp olive oil

½ tsp medium hot chili powder (optional)

salt

Barbecue Sauce (*see* page 132) or tomato ketchup, to serve

Preheat the oven to 200°C/400°F/Gas Mark 6. Cut each vegetable lengthways into 1-cm/½-inch thick slices, then cut each slice into 1-cm/½-inch fries. Toss the fries with the remaining ingredients, then arrange in a single layer in 1–2 baking dishes. Bake for 45 minutes, turning them over every 15 minutes until lightly browned and cooked. Serve with Barbecue Sauce or ketchup.

NACHO CHEESE POPCORN

Popcorn is such a great snack and this nacho popcorn tastes surprisingly cheesy!

Makes 1 large bowl

2 tbsp coconut oil

40 g/1½ oz/¼ cup popping corn

For the seasoning

2 tbsp coconut oil

1 garlic clove, peeled and crushed

2 tbsp nutritional yeast flakes

1 tsp lime juice

¼ tsp smoked paprika

½ tsp unrefined salt

Use a large pan and get the oil really hot. Add 3 popping corn kernels. Once they have popped, the oil is hot enough. Add the remaining corn. Cover, reduce the heat to low and cook until the corn stops popping, shaking the pan regularly. Once the popping stops, uncover.

Mix all the seasoning ingredients together. Add the popcorn and mix to coat.

LIGHT MEALS & SIDES

SEITAN BURRITO WRAPS

Making your own lunchtime wraps is much more satisfying and tasty than buying them. Seitan is available in most good health food shops.

Serves 1

For the guacamole

½ ripe avocado

½ lime

1 large pinch salt

For the Pico de Gallo

1 tomato, diced

2.5 cm/1 inch piece cucumber, diced

¼ small red onion, diced

1 tbsp chopped coriander (cilantro)

For the wrap

1 tbsp olive oil

2 seitan slices

1 large flour tortilla wrap

For the guacamole, mash the avocado with the lime and salt. For the Pico de Gallo, combine all the ingredients together.

For the wrap, heat the oil in a frying pan over a medium heat and fry the seitan for 3 minutes on each side. Lay the tortilla on a flat surface. Distribute the guacamole, Pico de Gallo and seitan over the wrap, leaving the ends bare. Roll up, folding in the ends to stop the filling falling out. Cut diagonally across the centre before serving.

JAPANESE TOFU SALAD SANDWICH

The Japanese-inspired marinade here is perfect for making a simple ingredient shine out, making lunch that bit more exotic!

Serves 1

½ tbsp tamari

½ tsp toasted sesame oil

½ tsp maple syrup

1 tsp rice vinegar

2 x 1-cm/½-inch tofu slices

2 tbsp vegetable oil

1 baby leek, sliced lengthways

1 large bread roll, halved

½ tomato, sliced

1 small handful lamb's lettuce (corn salad) or other lettuce

1 large gherkin (pickle), sliced

1 tsp sesame seeds

Combine the tamari, sesame oil, maple syrup and vinegar. Add the tofu and coat in the marinade. Leave to stand.

Heat the vegetable oil in a frying pan over a medium heat and fry the leek for 5–10 minutes. Remove from the pan, leaving the oil in the pan. Spread the bread roll with the leftover leek oil.

Fry the tofu in the marinade over a medium heat until the liquid has evaporated, flipping the tofu halfway through cooking. Layer the sandwich with the tomato, tofu, lettuce, gherkin (pickle), fried leeks and sesame seeds and serve.

CREAMY MUSHROOM SOUP

Using brown mushrooms will give your soup that lovely earthy colour. The freshness of the parsley contrasts nicely with the rich creaminess of the soup.

Makes 1 large or 2 smaller bowls

2 tbsp olive oil

8 chestnut (cremini) mushrooms, sliced

1 garlic clove, peeled and crushed

1 celery stalk, sliced

1 tbsp soy sauce or tamari

300 ml/10 fl oz/1¼ cups unsweetened almond milk

½ tbsp chopped flat-leaf parsley

Heat the oil in a pan and fry the mushrooms, garlic and celery until soft and cooked through.

Blend the soy sauce, milk and cooked vegetables until smooth and creamy. Return the soup to the pan and cook gently until steaming hot but not boiling. Serve topped with parsley.

RAINBOW SUMMER ROLLS

Rice sheets are available from Asian stores. Submerge each sheet in a bowl of hot water to soften it just before you are ready to use it. These rolls are delicious as a light lunch or colourful and sophisticated starter.

Serves 2 as a main dish or 4 as a starter

4 large rice sheets

75 g/3 oz/1 cup red cabbage, finely sliced

1 carrot, peeled and cut into julienne strips

1 red (bell) pepper, finely sliced

1 handful coriander (cilantro)

1 tbsp chia seeds (optional)

For the dipping sauce

4 tbsp soy sauce or tamari

1 tsp toasted sesame oil

2 tbsp rice vinegar

2 garlic cloves, peeled

1 mild red chili

4 pitted Medjool dates

For the dipping sauce, blend all the ingredients until smooth.

Prepare one roll at a time as follows:

* Carefully place a softened rice sheet on a flat surface.
* Layer red cabbage, carrot, pepper, coriander (cilantro) and chia seeds along the centre of the sheet, leaving 2.5 cm/1 inch free at the ends. Don't overfill.

- Roll into a tight sausage, encasing the filling and tucking the ends in to stop the filling from falling out.
- Repeat with the remaining rice sheets.

Once all the rolls are completed, carefully cut each one in half diagonally and arrange on a plate. Serve with the dipping sauce.

PIZZA PITTAS

Add extra toppings to these pizza pittas, such as red onion and peppers, and use a melty vegan cheese.

Makes 4

1 tbsp olive oil

1 garlic clove, peeled and crushed

100 g/3½ oz/scant ½ cup canned chopped tomatoes

2 sun-dried tomatoes, in oil or rehydrated, chopped

1 tsp dried oregano

pinch unrefined salt

pinch unrefined granulated sugar

4 pitta breads

2 large tomatoes, sliced

100 g/3½ oz/generous 1 cup grated vegan cheese

oregano leaves (optional)

Preheat the oven to 200°C/400°F/Gas Mark 6.

Heat the oil in a pan over a medium heat and cook the garlic for 1 minute. Add the chopped and sun-dried tomatoes, oregano, salt and sugar and cook for 10 minutes before blending to make a sauce.

Spread a layer of sauce on top of the pittas. Add the sliced tomato and vegan cheese and cook for 10–15 minutes. Top with oregano and serve.

FISHLESS TUNA PASTA SALAD

This satisfying salad is served with a vegan take on tuna.

Serves 4

400 g/14 oz/scant 3 cups canned chickpeas

56 g/2¼ oz/¼ cup vegan mayonnaise

1 tbsp Dijon mustard

1½ tbsp red wine vinegar

large pinch salt

100 g/3½ oz macaroni pasta

2 gherkins (pickles), sliced

2 tbsp olive oil

1 tbsp lemon juice

salt and freshly ground black pepper

1 tbsp chopped chives, for topping (optional)

Pulse the chickpeas in a food processor 2 or 3 times. Stir in the mayonnaise, mustard, vinegar and salt. Set aside.

Cook the macaroni in a pan according to the packet instructions. Drain and refresh in cold water. Combine the pasta with the gherkins (pickles), oil and lemon juice. Stir through the chickpea mix and season. Top with chives, if liked.

POTATO & RUNNER BEAN SALAD

Other fresh beans are wonderful with this salad too – try green beans or sugar snap peas for a different take.

Serves 2 as a main dish or 4 as a starter

450 g/1 lb (16 oz) potatoes, peeled
300 g/11 oz runner beans, cut into generous chunks

For the dressing

3 tbsp olive oil
2 bird's-eye (Thai) chilies (peppers), deseeded and cut into fat slices
1 shallot, peeled and sliced
1 rosemary sprig
pinch unrefined salt

Cook the potatoes in a pan of boiling water for 20 minutes until still firm but a knife pierces them easily. Drain, refresh in cold water and set aside.

Steam the beans for 10 minutes until tender, then refresh in cold water and set aside.

For the dressing, heat the oil in a pan over a medium heat and fry the remaining ingredients for 10 minutes until the shallot is soft.

Meanwhile, cut the potatoes into slices. Carefully combine the potato slices, beans and dressing and serve on a large plate.

THE BEST ROAST POTATOES EVER

The best roast potatoes are crispy and slightly browned on the outside, while being melt-in-the-mouth on the inside. Although this method is quite involved, it is worth the effort as it produces the best roast potatoes ever!

Serves 2 as a side dish

900 g/2 lb roasting potatoes, peeled and cut into 5 x 5-cm/2 x 2-inch chunks
200 ml/7 fl oz/scant 1 cup vegetable oil
8 garlic cloves
1 rosemary sprig
salt

Preheat the oven to 240°/475°F/Gas Mark 9.

Parboil the potatoes in a pan of boiling water for 10 minutes, then drain and return to the pan, cover and toss to fluff the outsides.

Add the oil to a large baking pan and heat in the oven until the oil is very hot. Add the potatoes to the hot oil in a single layer. Baste the potatoes in oil and roast for 15 minutes until they just start to brown.

Remove the potatoes from the oven and turn each one over, adding the garlic, rosemary and salt.

Reduce the heat to 200°C/400°F/Gas Mark 6 and roast the potatoes for another 45 minutes, turning them over every 15 minutes, until gorgeously brown and crispy.

COMFORT FOOD

SPAGHETTI PUTTANESCA

Puttanesca is a deeply flavourful and traditional Italian pasta dish, with a bit of fire in the sauce.

Serves 2

165 g/5½ oz spaghetti

3 tbsp olive oil

2 garlic cloves, peeled and crushed

½ tsp chili flakes

50 g/2 oz/generous ⅓ cup pitted mixed olives

1½ tbsp rinsed capers

1 tsp dried oregano

300 g/11 oz/1¼ cups canned chopped tomatoes

2 tbsp tomato purée (paste)

salt and freshly ground black pepper

To serve

green salad

crusty bread

Cook the spaghetti according to the packet instructions.

Meanwhile, heat the oil in a large frying pan over a medium-low heat and fry the garlic, chili flakes, olives, capers and oregano for 2 minutes. Add the tomatoes and tomato purée (paste) and bring to the boil. Reduce the heat and simmer until the pasta is ready.

Drain the pasta and return it to the pan. Season the sauce, then add half the sauce, mostly without olives, to the pasta and mix it through. Divide among bowls, top with the remaining sauce and serve with a green salad and bread.

BEST VEGGIE BURGER EVER

Nothing beats a good veggie burger. This one is packed full of goodness and tastes amazing too.

Makes 2

For the herb salsa

3 tbsp chopped parsley

3 tbsp chopped oregano

1 tbsp olive oil

2 tsp lemon juice

large pinch salt

For the burgers

3 tbsp olive oil

2 garlic cloves, peeled and crushed

1 tsp ground cumin

1 tsp smoked paprika

300 g/11 oz/generous 2 cups cooked chickpeas, mashed

1 tbsp ground flaxseed

¼ tsp salt

For the best veggie burger ever!

2 ciabatta buns, or your favourite burger bun

2 tbsp vegan mayonnaise

1 handful baby spinach

6 cucumber slices

1 handful alfalfa sprouts

½ avocado, sliced

For the salsa, mix all the ingredients together and set aside.

For the burgers, heat 1 tablespoon of the oil in a frying pan and fry the garlic and spices for 1 minute. Stir in the chickpeas with the ground flaxseed and salt, then roughly mix in 4 tablespoons of the salsa. Make 2 patties and fry them in the remaining oil for 5 minutes on each side until browned.

Cut the rolls in half and spread with mayonnaise and the remaining salsa. Add spinach, cucumber, alfalfa sprouts, avocado and a burger and serve.

CAULIFLOWER MAC `N` CHEEZE

Vegan mac n' cheese – yes it's possible and totally delicious! This classic comfort food is a favourite with kids and grown-ups alike.

Serves 4

1 small cauliflower, cut into florets

200 g/7 oz macaroni pasta

2 quantities Cheeze Sauce (*see* page 136)

crusty bread or roast potatoes (*see* page 160), to serve

Preheat the oven to 180°C/350°F/Gas Mark 4.

Steam the cauliflower for 15 minutes.

Cook the macaroni in a pan of boiling water according to the packet instructions.

Meanwhile, prepare the Cheeze Sauce according to page 136.

Once everything is ready, mix them together, then transfer to a baking dish and bake for 30–40 minutes until browned. Serve with bread or potatoes.

LENTIL TACOS

Serve these lovely tacos with guacamole and Pico de Gallo (*see* page 144) for a comforting lunch or relaxed supper.

Serves 2

2 tbsp vegetable oil

1 onion, peeled and diced

2 garlic cloves, peeled and crushed

1 tsp ground cumin

1 tsp ground coriander

½ tsp mild chili powder

250 g/9 oz/1¼ cups cooked green lentils

50 g/2 oz/⅓ cup cooked kidney beans

¼ tsp unrefined salt

4 taco shells

coriander (cilantro) leaves, for sprinkling

Heat the oil in a pan and fry the onion until soft. Add the garlic and spices and cook for 1 minute. Stir in the lentils, beans and salt and cook over a medium heat for 5 minutes until the beans are hot. Spoon the mixture into tacos and top with coriander (cilantro).

CANNELLINI, KALE & FARRO SOUP

Farro refers to an ancient wheat species, also known as emmer. It has a nutty flavour similar to brown rice. If you can't find farro, use barley groats instead.

Serves 4

100 g/3½ oz/½ cup farro

2 tbsp olive oil

1 onion, peeled and diced

3 garlic cloves, peeled and crushed

1 rosemary sprig, leaves only

1 carrot, peeled and diced

½ red (bell) pepper, diced

2 celery stalks, diced

100 g/3½ oz/1½ cups kale, shredded

200 g/7 oz/generous ¾ cup canned chopped tomatoes

1 litre/1¾ pints/4 cups water

salt and freshly ground black pepper

200 g/7 oz/scant 1½ cups cooked cannellini beans

125 ml/4 fl oz/½ cup unsweetened almond milk

crusty bread, to serve

Soak the farro in plenty of room temperature water.

Heat the oil in a pan over a low heat and cook the onion for 10 minutes. Add the garlic and rosemary and cook for 1 minute. Add the diced vegetables, kale and tomatoes, cover and sweat over a medium-low heat for 5 minutes.

Add the farro, water and ½ teaspoon salt and bring to the boil. Reduce the heat, cover and simmer for 20–30 minutes until the farro is cooked.

Stir in the beans and milk and season. Cook for 10 minutes until the beans are hot. Serve with bread.

CHILI & RICE

This is also delicious served with a dollop of vegan yogurt on top.

Serves 2

3 tbsp olive oil

1 onion, peeled and diced

6 mushrooms, sliced

1 red (bell) pepper, cored, deseeded and diced

2 garlic cloves, peeled and crushed

½ tsp medium-hot chili powder

1 tsp smoked paprika

1 tsp ground cumin

2 tsp dried oregano

400 g/14 oz/1⅔ cups canned chopped tomatoes

200 g/7 oz/generous 1¼ cups cooked red kidney beans

1 tbsp lime juice

pinch unrefined granulated sugar

¼ tsp unrefined salt

150 g/5 oz/generous ¾ cup white rice

Heat the oil in a pan over a medium heat and cook the onion for 5 minutes. Add the mushrooms and pepper and cook for 5 minutes. Mix in the garlic, spices and oregano and cook for 1 minute. Add the canned tomatoes, beans, lime juice, sugar and salt, bring to the boil, reduce the heat and simmer, uncovered, for 20 minutes.

Cook the rice according to the packet instructions. Serve, the rice topped with chili.

SPAGHETTI WITH MEATLESS BALLS

Spaghetti is one of the best comfort foods. This is a great recipe for a cosy supper, or if you're having friends round for a lazy weekend lunch. TVP (textured vegetable protein) is available from most good health food stores.

Serves 2

165 g/5½oz dried spaghetti

2 tbsp olive oil, for cooking the balls

finely chopped basil leaves, to garnish

For the meatless balls

100 g/3½ oz TVP

2 garlic cloves, peeled and crushed

3 tbsp soy sauce

2 tsp dried oregano

½ tsp ground cumin

250 ml/8 fl oz/1 cup boiling water

For the tomato sauce

2 tbsp olive oil

1 onion, peeled and diced

3 garlic cloves, peeled and crushed

400 g/14 oz/1⅔ cups canned chopped tomatoes

¼ tsp salt

10 pitted green olives, sliced

Stir all the meatless balls ingredients together and leave for 15 minutes.

For the sauce, heat the oil in a pan over a medium heat and fry the onion for 5 minutes. Add the garlic and fry for 1 minute. Add the tomatoes, salt and olives. Bring to the boil, reduce the heat and simmer, uncovered, for 20 minutes.

Chop the TVP mixture in a food processor. Using your hands, form the mixture into small balls and set aside.

Cook the spaghetti in a pan of boiling water according to the packet instructions.

Heat the oil for cooking the balls in a frying pan over a medium heat and fry the balls for 3 minutes on each side until browned.

Stir the sauce through the spaghetti and top with the meatless balls and basil.

AUBERGINE FRITTERS

Vegetable fritters usually rely on egg for the batter. Here, we replace egg with ground flaxseed.

Serves 2

2 aubergines (eggplants), cut into 2-cm/¾-inch slices

salt, for sprinkling

150 g/5 oz/3⅓ cups white breadcrumbs

2 tbsp nutritional yeast flakes

1 tbsp lemon juice

2 garlic cloves, peeled and crushed

1 tbsp dried oregano

¼ tsp unrefined salt

4 tbsp ground flaxseed

175 ml/6 fl oz/¾ cup water

125 ml/4 fl oz/½ cup olive oil, for frying

To serve

Barbecue Sauce (*see* page 132)

salad

Place the aubergine (eggplant) slices in a colander in the sink. Sprinkle generously with salt and leave for 30 minutes.

Preheat the oven to 110°C/225°F/Gas Mark ¼.

Combine the breadcrumbs, yeast flakes, lemon juice, garlic, oregano and salt in a bowl.

In another bowl, mix the ground flaxseed with the water to make flax egg.

Rinse the aubergine and pat dry with paper towels.

Dip each aubergine slice into the flax egg, then into the breadcrumb mix to coat, then place on a plate, separated by greaseproof (wax) paper.

Heat 1 cm/½ inch olive oil in a large frying pan until very hot. Reduce the heat to medium and fry the aubergine slices for 7–10 minutes on each side until browned. Place the cooked slices between layers of paper towel and keep warm in the oven while you fry the next batch.

Serve with Barbecue Sauce and salad.

DINNER PARTY
DISHES

THAI GREEN CURRY

Thai green curry is divine, especially with freshly made curry paste. Be aware that many vegetarian stock cubes contain whey from milk.

Serves 4

150 g/5 oz/generous ¾ cup black rice

1 bay leaf

200 g/7 oz chestnut (cremini) mushrooms, quartered

400 ml/14 fl oz/1¾ cups canned coconut milk

200 ml/7 fl oz/scant 1 cup vegan stock

2 tbsp soy sauce

200 g/7 oz green beans, trimmed

400 g/14 oz tofu, cubed

75 g/3 oz/⅔ cup frozen petit pois

1 handful Thai basil leaves

For the paste

6 kaffir lime leaves

1 mild green chili, deseeded

2 lemongrass stalks, tough layers removed

2.5 cm/1 inch ginger root

2 garlic cloves

2 handfuls coriander (cilantro)

4 spring onions (scallions)

50 ml/2 fl oz/¼ cup melted coconut oil

Cook the black rice according to the packet instructions. For the paste, blitz all the ingredients in a small food processor or use a handheld blender.

Fry the paste in a pan over a medium-low heat for 1 minute. Add the bay leaf and mushrooms and cook for 5 minutes.

Add the milk, stock, soy sauce and beans and bring to the boil. Add the tofu and petit pois and return to the boil.

Reduce the heat and simmer for 5–7 minutes. Stir through the basil and serve.

SPINACH & MUSHROOM PANCAKES
with Béchamel Sauce

This sophisticated supper dish is in three parts. You can make each of the three recipes in advance, freezing the pancakes and the filling to save time. Serve with a simple green salad.

Serves 2

For the filling

200 g/7 oz spinach

1 tbsp olive oil

1 onion, peeled and diced

2 garlic cloves, peeled and crushed

200 g/7 oz chestnut (cremini) mushrooms, sliced

¼ tsp salt

For the sauce

300 ml/10 fl oz/1¼ cups unsweetened soya milk

2 tbsp vegetable oil

2 tbsp plain (all-purpose) flour

salt and freshly ground black pepper

For the pancakes

50 g/2 oz/generous ⅓ cup plain (all-purpose) flour

1 tbsp ground flaxseed

150 ml/5 fl oz/⅔ cup unsweetened soya milk

2 tsp vegetable oil

pinch salt

Steam the spinach for 5 minutes. Set a small handful of spinach aside, squeezing the rest to remove excess liquid. Heat the oil in a pan and sauté the onion for 10 minutes until translucent. Add the garlic and cook for 1 minute, then add the mushrooms and salt and cook until soft. Keep warm.

For the sauce, gently scald the milk in a pan without boiling. Mix the oil and flour together in a small pan and cook for 2 minutes, stirring. Remove from the heat and mix in the hot milk. Bring the sauce to the boil, stirring. Reduce the heat and simmer for 2 minutes. Season.

Blend the pancake ingredients until smooth, then cook the pancakes according to the recipe on page 88.

Preheat the grill (broiler) to medium. Spoon some of the filling along the centre of each pancake, roll up and place in a small ovenproof dish. Top with the remaining spinach and sauce and grill for a few minutes until browned.

VEGAN NUT ROAST

You can't beat a good vegan Sunday roast! Team it up with steamed vegetables, roast parsnips, the Best Roast Potatoes Ever (*see* page 160) and vegan gravy.

Serves 4

1 tbsp vegetable oil, plus extra for oiling

1 large onion, peeled and diced

1 tsp ground cumin

100 ml/3½ fl oz/⅓ cup boiling water

1 vegan stock (bouillon) cube

1 heaped tsp yeast extract

225 g/8 oz/1½ cups mixed nuts, including the brazil nuts, finely chopped

40 g/1½ oz/⅓ cup grated carrot

100 g/3½ oz wholemeal (wholegrain) bread, blitzed into breadcrumbs

salt and freshly ground black pepper

Preheat the oven to 180°C/350°F/Gas Mark 4. Oil a 450-g/1-lb loaf tin.

Heat the oil in a frying pan over a low heat and cook the onions and cumin for 10 minutes until the onions are translucent.

Mix the boiling water with the stock (bouillon) cube and yeast extract in a heatproof jug. Add to the pan and bring to the boil.

Mix the chopped nuts, grated carrot and breadcrumbs together in a large bowl. Add the stock to make a mixture that is sticky but not wet. If the mixture doesn't stick together, add 1 tablespoon boiling water at a time until it holds together. Season to taste. Press and flatten firmly into the tin and bake for 25–35 minutes until browned on top. Serve.

CHEEZY LEEK TARTS

Impress your friends with these gorgeous tarts. They make a lovely starter, or a sophisticated main course served with a selection of salads.

Makes 4 tarts

vegetable oil, for oiling

225 g/8 oz/scant 1¾ cups plain (all-purpose) flour, plus extra for dusting

pinch salt

100 g/3½ oz/scant ½ cup cold vegan margarine, cubed

2½ tbsp cold water

For the cheezy leek filling

1 small leek, trimmed and finely sliced

1 tbsp olive oil

65 g/2½ oz/½ cup cashew nuts

1 tbsp nutritional yeast flakes

1 spring onion (scallion), chopped

1 tbsp lemon juice

½ tsp salt

85 ml/3 fl oz/generous ⅓ cup water

For the topping

½ courgette (zucchini), finely sliced

olive oil, for brushing

grated melty vegan cheese (optional)

Preheat the oven to 190°C/375°F/Gas Mark 5. Lightly oil four 8-cm/3¼-inch loose-based mini tart tins.

Mix the flour and salt in a bowl. Lightly rub in the margarine with your fingertips until it resembles soft breadcrumbs. Sprinkle the water over and mix with a knife to form a dough. Alternatively, use a food processor. Lightly form the dough into a ball, cover and refrigerate for at least 2 hours or overnight.

For the filling, set aside 4 leek slices. Heat the oil in a pan over a medium heat and sauté the remaining leeks for 5–10 minutes until cooked and slightly sweet. Blend the cashews, yeast flakes, spring onion (scallion), lemon juice, salt and water until smooth. Stir in the leeks and set aside.

Roll out the dough on a lightly floured surface to 3 mm/⅛ inch thick. Line each tart tin generously with the dough, leaving an overhang on each one. Blind bake the cases (shells) for 15 minutes, then remove from the oven, trim the pastry and cool.

Fill the pastry cases with the filling. Top with fans of courgette (zucchini) and reserved leek slices brushed with oil. Sprinkle the vegan cheese lightly over the top, if using, and bake for 15–20 minutes until golden on top.

POTATO DAUPHINOISE

Serve this alongside the Cheezy Leek Tarts (*see* page 190) or instead of roast potatoes.

Serves 8

3 garlic cloves, peeled

500 ml/18 fl oz/2 cups soy cream

500 ml/18 fl oz/2 cups unsweetened almond or soya milk

large pinch salt

8 large King Edward or Maris Piper potatoes, peeled and very thinly sliced, about
 3 mm/⅛ inch thick

Preheat the oven to 190°C/375°F/Gas Mark 5.

Gently squash the garlic with the back of a wooden spoon. Put the cream, milk, garlic and salt into a large pan and bring to a simmer. Add the potatoes and simmer, gently stirring, for 3 minutes until just cooked.

Remove the potatoes with a slotted spoon and place them in a shallow ovenproof dish so that they are about 5 cm/2 inches in depth. Discard the garlic from the sauce and pour over the potatoes, just enough to cover all the slices. Bake for 30 minutes until the potatoes are soft and browned on top.

Tip

Freeze any extra sauce for adding to soup or pasta dishes.

ITALIAN BAKE

If you have never tried a dish with a breadcrumb topping, you are in for a treat. The rosemary, oregano and thyme complement the sweetness of the roasted tomatoes and peppers beautifully.

Serves 4

For the topping

6 slices stale bread

1 tbsp thyme leaves

¼ tsp unrefined salt

1 tbsp olive oil

1 tsp lemon zest

1 tbsp lemon juice

For the vegetables

2 tbsp olive oil

1 medium onion, peeled and diced

4 garlic cloves, peeled and crushed

1 tbsp dried oregano

1 tbsp dried or fresh rosemary

¼ tsp salt

pinch unrefined granulated sugar

900 g/2 lb cherry tomatoes

1 orange (bell) pepper, cored, deseeded and diced

green salad, to serve

Preheat the oven to 180°C/350°F/Gas Mark 4.

For the topping, blitz all the ingredients together in a food processor until the bread becomes breadcrumbs. Set aside.

Combine all the remaining ingredients in an ovenproof dish and roast for 15 minutes. Remove from the oven and turn the vegetables. Top with the breadcrumb mixture and cook for 30 minutes until browned and crispy. Serve with salad.

COCONUT DHAL & PILAU RICE

Dhal and rice may seem like a simple dish, but the depth of flavour created by the spices make it a favourite with anyone who loves Indian food.

Serves 2

For the coconut dhal

1 tbsp coconut oil

1 tsp mustard seeds

½ tsp cumin seeds

1 tsp ground turmeric

1 tsp ground coriander

1 small onion, peeled and diced

1 large dried red chili

1 tomato, chopped

100 g/3½ oz/½ cup dried red lentils

200 ml/7 fl oz/scant 1 cup coconut milk

125 ml/4 fl oz/½ cup water

large pinch salt

For the pilau rice

2 tbsp vegetable oil

1 small onion, peeled and finely sliced

1 tsp cumin seeds

6 cardamom pods

1 cinnamon stick

3 cloves

150 g/5 oz/generous ¾ cup basmati rice

300 ml/10 fl oz/1¼ cups water

For the topping

1 tbsp coriander (cilantro) leaves
hot red chili sauce (optional)

For the dhal, heat the coconut oil and mustard seeds in a pan with the lid on. When the mustard seeds start to pop, add the spices and onion and cook over a medium heat for 5–10 minutes. Add the remaining ingredients. Bring to the boil, stirring frequently. Reduce the heat and simmer for 35 minutes, stirring occasionally.

For the rice, heat the vegetable oil until it is very hot and fry the onion until brown and crispy. Remove the onion and set aside. Add the spices and fry over a medium heat for 1 minute. Add the rice and fry for 2 minutes, stirring. Add the water, bring to the boil, reduce the heat, cover and simmer for 10 minutes until the rice is cooked.

Serve the dhal on a bed of rice, topped with coriander (cilantro) and red chili sauce, if liked.

SPANAKOPITA

Spanakopita is a Greek dish that is traditionally made with egg and feta. Here is the vegan version! Serve with Tzatziki (see page 130) and a green salad.

Serves 6 as a main or 12 as a starter

For the filling

500 g/1 lb 1 oz fresh spinach

2 tbsp ground flaxseed

2 tbsp olive oil

1 large onion, peeled and finely chopped

2 garlic cloves, peeled and very finely chopped

pinch grated nutmeg

300 g/11 oz/3 cups ground Brazil nuts

2 tbsp nutritional yeast flakes

2 tbsp lemon juice

½ tsp salt

2 tsp chopped dill

freshly ground black pepper

For the filo top

250 ml/8 fl oz/1 cup olive oil, for oiling and brushing

450 g/1 lb ready-made filo (phyllo) pastry sheets

Submerge the spinach in boiling water for 5 minutes. Drain and squeeze out any excess liquid, saving 6 tablespoons juice. Mix the saved juice with the ground flaxseed to make flax egg.

Heat the oil in a pan and cook the onion until translucent. Add the garlic and cook for 1 minute.

Remove the pan from the heat and mix in all the remaining filling ingredients. Add pepper to taste.

Preheat the oven to 190°C/375°F/Gas Mark 5. Brush a 24 x 32-cm/9½ x 13-inch metal baking pan with oil.

Lay the filo (phyllo) between 2 slightly damp tea (dish) towels to stop it drying. Lay a filo sheet over the bottom and sides of the baking dish, leaving an overhang of pastry. Brush with oil. Turn the dish slightly and add 3 more sheets, brushing with oil and turning the dish between sheets.

Spoon the filling evenly into the baking pan. Fold the overhang of pastry over the filling. Top with 8 more layers of filo cut to fit the top of the baking pan, brushing each layer with oil. Brush the top layer with oil and score with a sharp knife. Bake for 1 hour, or until the pastry is crisp and golden.

CAKES, TREATS & DESSERTS

CHOCOLATE HAZELNUT CRÊPES

Chocolate-filled crêpes are such a treat! Keep a jar of this spread in your cupboard and you'll be ready at a moment's notice to whip up these delicious delights.

Makes 8 crêpes

2 tbsp ground flaxseed

350 ml/12 fl oz/1½ cups unsweetened dairy-free milk

75 g/3 oz/½ cup plain (all-purpose) flour

pinch salt

1½ tsp vegetable oil, plus extra for brushing

For the chocolate hazelnut spread (makes 250 ml/8 fl oz/1 cup)

125 ml/4 fl oz/scant ⅔ cup coconut oil

6 tbsp unsweetened cocoa powder

6 tbsp maple syrup

50 g/2 oz/½ cup ground toasted hazelnuts (grind in a spice grinder or
   high-speed blender)

1 tsp vanilla extract

pinch salt

For the spread, melt the coconut oil in a heatproof bowl set over just-boiled water. Stir in the remaining ingredients and mix until smooth. Spoon into a sterilized jar.

To make the crêpes, combine the ground flaxseed, milk, flour, salt and vegetable oil in a blender until smooth. Cover and chill for 1 hour.

Heat a frying pan over a medium-high heat and brush with vegetable oil. Pour 50 ml/ 2 fl oz/¼ cup of the batter into the pan, tilting to coat the surface of the pan and cook for 1–2 minutes until golden. Carefully flip and cook for another 1–2 minutes. Repeat with the remaining batter.

Spread 2 tablespoons of the chocolate hazelnut spread onto each crêpe, fold into quarters and serve in a pretty pile.

STRAWBERRY CHEESECAKE POTS

To prepare in advance, follow the recipe until the topping, then freeze. Remove from the freezer 4–8 hours before eating, adding the fruit topping.

Makes 4

For the base

2 Shortbreads (*see* page 212) or plain vegan biscuits, broken into fine crumbs
pinch salt

For the filling

130 g/4½ oz/1 cup cashew nuts
2 tsp lemon zest (about 1 lemon)
2 tbsp lemon juice
3 tbsp melted coconut oil
50 ml/2 fl oz/¼ cup water
1 tbsp vanilla extract
1 tsp maple syrup
½ tsp nutritional yeast flakes (optional)

For the topping

6 tbsp good strawberry jam
2 tbsp water
6 fresh strawberries, sliced
mint leaves, to decorate (optional)

For the base, divide the biscuit crumbs evenly among 4 small glasses or jars and firm down using the back of a teaspoon.

For the filling, blend all the ingredients until smooth and creamy. Spoon on top of the bases.

For the topping, mix the strawberry jam and water together. Pour a thin layer on top of each filling. Top with strawberries and pour the remaining jam over. Add a mint sprig, if liked, and chill for 1 hour.

CHOCOLATE MOUSSE
with Peanut Brittle

If you don't fancy making the peanut brittle, use a good-quality store-bought brand instead.

Serves 2

For the peanut brittle

coconut oil, for oiling

200 g/7 oz/1 cup unrefined granulated sugar

50 ml/2 fl oz/¼ cup water

pinch salt

100 g/3½ oz/¾ cup salted peanuts

vegetable oil, for spatula

For the mousse

1 ripe avocado

3 heaped tsp unsweetened cocoa powder

2 tbsp maple syrup

small pinch salt

½ tsp vanilla extract

100 ml/3½ fl oz/⅓ cup water

For the peanut brittle, grease a baking sheet with coconut oil and keep warm in a low oven.

Stir the sugar, water and salt in a pan and cook over a high heat, without stirring, for 3 minutes until the sugar begins to dissolve. Reduce the heat to medium and cook for 10 minutes, stirring occasionally, until the sugar has dissolved and turned a deep gold. Don't let it burn. Remove from the heat. Stir in the peanuts, pour the mixture onto the baking sheet and quickly spread to 1 cm/½ inch thick using an oiled spatula. Cool completely before breaking into rough pieces.

For the mousse, blend all the ingredients together until mousse-like.

Decorate the mousse with brittle. There is no need to chill to set; you can refrigerate for up to 24 hours, but it will start to discolour after 4 hours.

SHORTBREAD

Traditionally, shortbread contains a lot of butter. In this recipe, we use coconut oil to give these biscuits their rich deliciousness. Serve them with coffee or with vegan ice cream and strawberries.

Makes about 10 biscuits

200 g/7 oz/1½ cups plain (all-purpose) flour, plus extra for dusting
50 g/2 oz/¼ cup caster (superfine) sugar, plus extra for sprinkling
generous pinch salt
100 g/3½ oz/½ cup coconut oil

Preheat the oven to 170°C/325°F/Gas Mark 3 and line a rimmed baking sheet with greaseproof (wax) paper.

Mix the flour, sugar and salt together in a bowl. Rub in the oil with your fingertips until the mixture resembles soft breadcrumbs. Press together and flatten the dough out on greaseproof (wax) paper to 1 cm/½ inch thick, then cut out shapes with a cookie cutter. Using a spatula, gently move each biscuit to the baking sheet. Repeat until all the dough is used up.

Sprinkle with sugar, then bake for 20–30 minutes until pale golden. Leave on the baking sheet to cool completely before storing in an airtight container for up to 2 weeks in the refrigerator.

CHOCOLATE FUDGE CAKE

Who doesn't love a good chocolate fudge cake? Make it at the weekend to impress your friends or to celebrate a birthday. No one will know it's vegan!

Makes 12 slices

For the cake

500 ml/18 fl oz/2 cups unsweetened dairy-free milk

150 ml/5 fl oz/⅔ cup melted coconut oil or light vegetable oil

2 tsp vanilla extract

325 g/11½ oz/2½ cups plain (all-purpose) flour

400 g/14 oz/2 cups unrefined granulated sugar

75 g/3 oz/¾ cup unsweetened cocoa powder

1 tsp salt

1 tsp cider vinegar

2 tsp bicarbonate of soda (baking soda)

For the frosting

125 ml/4 fl oz/½ cup melted coconut oil

125 ml/4 fl oz/½ cup water

1 tbsp vanilla extract

300 g/11 oz/2 cups avocado, cubed

50 g/2 oz/½ cup unsweetened cocoa powder

100 g/3½ oz/1 cup icing (confectioners') sugar

2 pinches salt

Preheat the oven to 180°C/350°F/Gas Mark 4. Line two 20-cm/8-inch cake tins with greaseproof (wax) paper.

Blend all the cake ingredients, except the vinegar and bicarbonate of soda (baking soda) until smooth. Add the vinegar and bicarbonate of soda and blend for just long enough to mix into the batter. Do not over-blend or your cake will not rise well.

Divide the batter between the tins and bake for 30–40 minutes. After 30 minutes, test the cake by inserting a sharp knife or skewer – if it comes out with cake batter on it, cook for another 10 minutes.

Leave the cakes to stand for 10 minutes, then remove from their tins and cool on a wire rack. Cut the domed top off one of the cakes to make it flat.

Blend all the frosting ingredients together until smooth and creamy. Using a spatula, spread a generous layer of frosting on top of the flattened cake. Place the second cake on top and spread the remaining frosting over the cake.

Best eaten on the day of making, but will keep in a sealed container in the refrigerator for up to 3 days.

LEMON POPPY SEED CAKE

This divine cake works equally well with a cup of tea mid-morning, or as a refreshing dessert with ice cream and fruit. If you prefer your cake round, use a cake tin instead.

Makes 12 slices

125 ml/4 fl oz/½ cup light vegetable oil, e.g. canola or sunflower oil, plus extra for oiling

300 ml/10 fl oz/1¼ cups unsweetened almond or soya milk

grated zest of 2 lemons

100 ml/3½ fl oz/⅓ cup lemon juice

1 tsp vanilla extract

250 g/9 oz/2 cups plain (all-purpose) flour

150 g/5 oz/¾ cup unrefined granulated sugar

1 tsp baking powder

½ tsp bicarbonate of soda (baking soda)

¼ tsp salt

3 tbsp poppy seeds

Preheat the oven to 190°C/375°F/Gas Mark 5. Lightly oil a 450-g/1-lb loaf tin with vegetable oil.

Whisk the milk, vegetable oil, lemon zest, lemon juice and vanilla together.

In another bowl, mix the dry ingredients together.

Pour the wet ingredients into the dry and stir until just combined. Don't over-mix! Pour into the tin and bake for 45–55 minutes, rotating once midway through. Insert a knife or skewer into the cake to test if it is ready – if it comes out clean, it is cooked; if it comes out with batter on it, cook for another 10 minutes.

STICKY MANGO RICE PUDDING

This is one of my all-time favourite desserts! It's fruity and comforting and the perfect accompaniment to the Thai green curry on page 184.

Serves 2

100 g/3½ oz/½ cup sticky rice (sushi rice)

85 ml/3 fl oz/⅓ cup coconut milk

1 tbsp unrefined granulated sugar

pinch salt

1 tbsp toasted coconut, to decorate

For the poached mango

1 large ripe mango

750 ml/1¼ pints/3 cups water

100 g/3½ oz/½ cup unrefined granulated sugar

2 cinnamon sticks

6 cardamom pods, crushed

Soak the rice in cold water for at least 3 hours, or overnight. Drain and rinse thoroughly. Line the steaming tier of a steamer pan with double thickness muslin (cheesecloth) or a clean tea (dish) towel and place the rice on top. Fill the base of the steamer with 5 cm/2 inches water, put the rice on top and bring to the boil. Steam the rice over a medium heat for 30 minutes, using a spoon to turn the rice halfway through.

Combine the coconut milk and sugar in a small pan and heat gently, stirring, until the sugar has dissolved. Do not boil. Stir in the salt and pour over the cooked rice, gently mixing the two together. Cool.

For the poached mango, peel the mango and slice the two fat cheeks off the fruit as close to the stone as possible.

Gently heat the remaining poached mango ingredients in a pan, stirring until the sugar is dissolved. Place the mango in the liquid with a plate on top to keep the fruit submerged. Bring to the boil, then reduce the heat and simmer for 15 minutes. Remove from the heat and slice the mango. Divide between 2 bowls and top with the coconut rice and a sprinkling of toasted coconut.

APPLE & BERRY CRUMBLE
with Custard

This pudding is lovely when it is made in individual heatproof bowls, but you can use one larger heatproof dish instead. Serve with Custard (*see* page 80) or yogurt.

Serves 4

For the dried apple

1 eating apple

For the filling

4 peeled and cored eating apples

350 g/12 oz/2½ cups frozen or fresh mixed berries

65 g/2½ oz/⅓ cup unrefined granulated sugar

1 tsp vanilla extract

For the crumble

125 g/4 oz/1 cup plain (all-purpose) flour

50 g/2 oz/¼ cup caster (superfine) sugar, plus extra for sprinkling

2 tbsp melted coconut oil

pinch salt

1 tsp ground cinnamon

Preheat the oven to 95°C/200°F/Gas Mark ¼. For the dried apple, finely slice the apple across its body with a large sharp knife or mandoline. Place the slices on greaseproof (wax) paper on a rimmed baking sheet and bake for 2–3 hours. Turn the oven off and leave them to cool in the oven for another hour.

For the filling, preheat the oven to 190°C/375°F/Gas Mark 5. Cut the apples into bite-size chunks. Set aside a handful of berries for topping, then mix the remaining berries with the apple chunks, sugar and vanilla. Divide the fruit mix between 4 heatproof bowls.

To make the topping, mix the flour, sugar, oil, salt and cinnamon together in a bowl. Sprinkle over the filling. Scatter a few berries on top and sprinkle with a little more sugar.

Place the bowls on a rimmed baking sheet and cook in the oven for 35 minutes until golden. Top with dried apple. Serve hot.

INDEX

Entries with upper-case initials indicate recipes.